Flower Power

Coloring the Sixties

Little Tree Artistry Series

AI Assisted Creation

Printed in the United States of America

ISBN 9798883648976

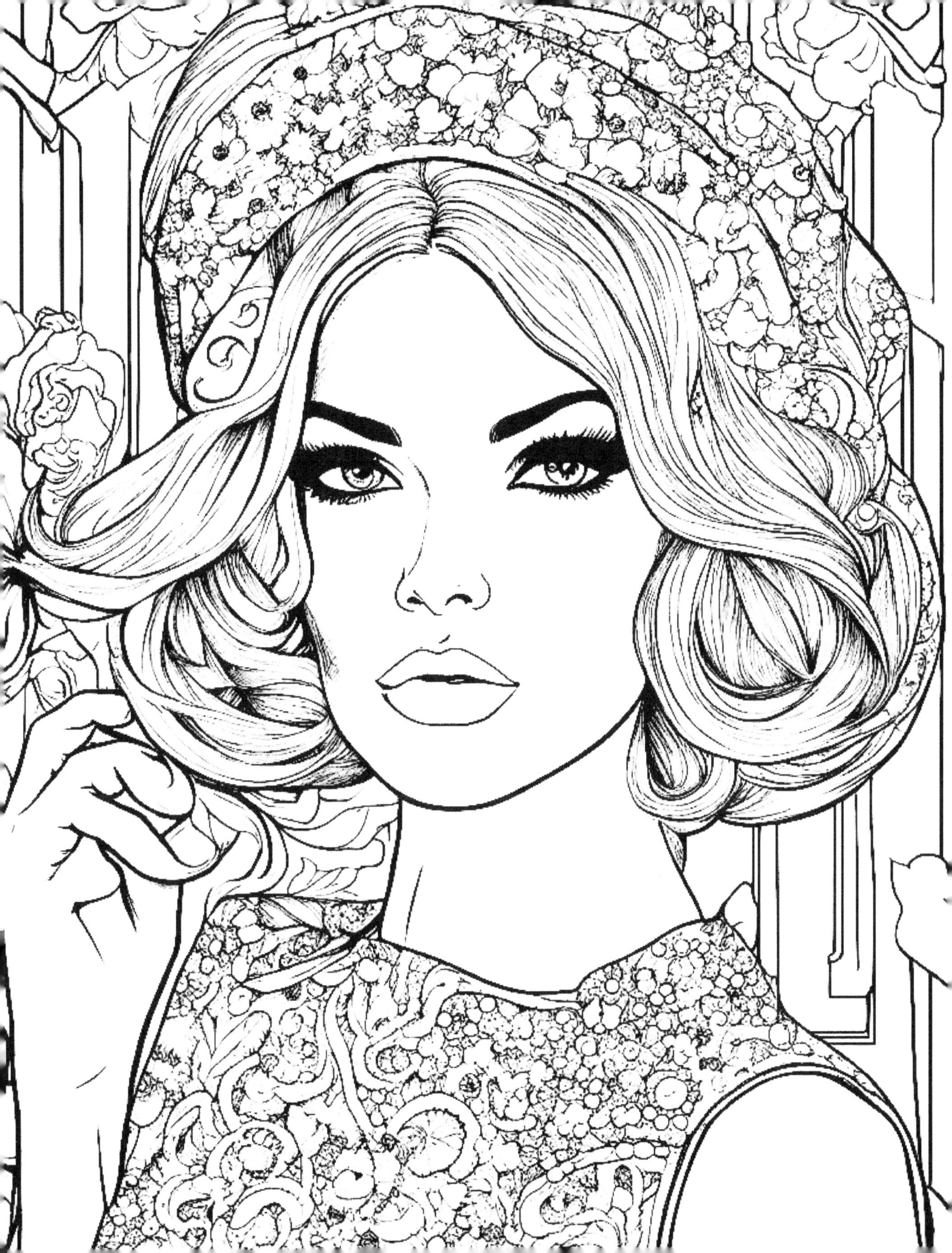

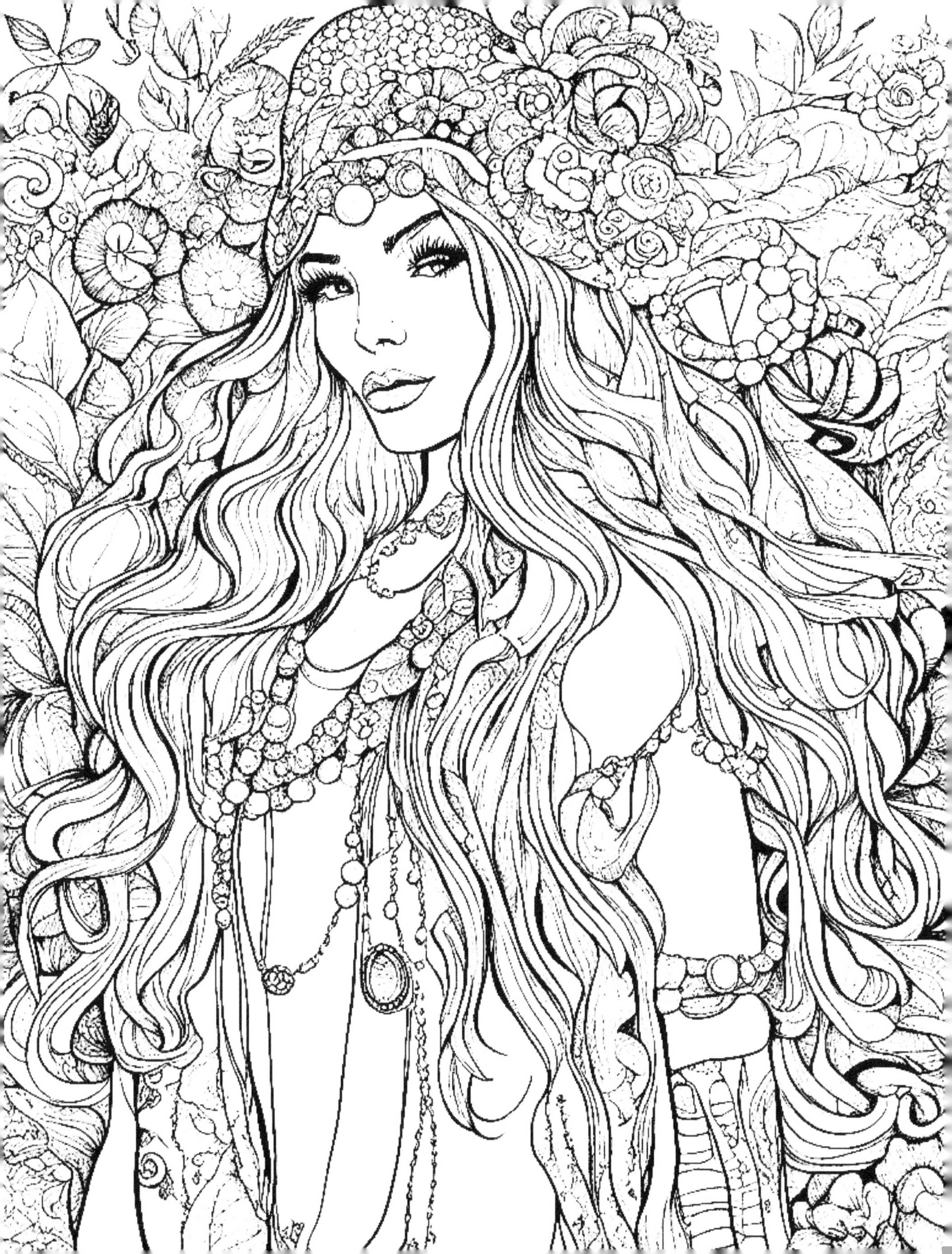

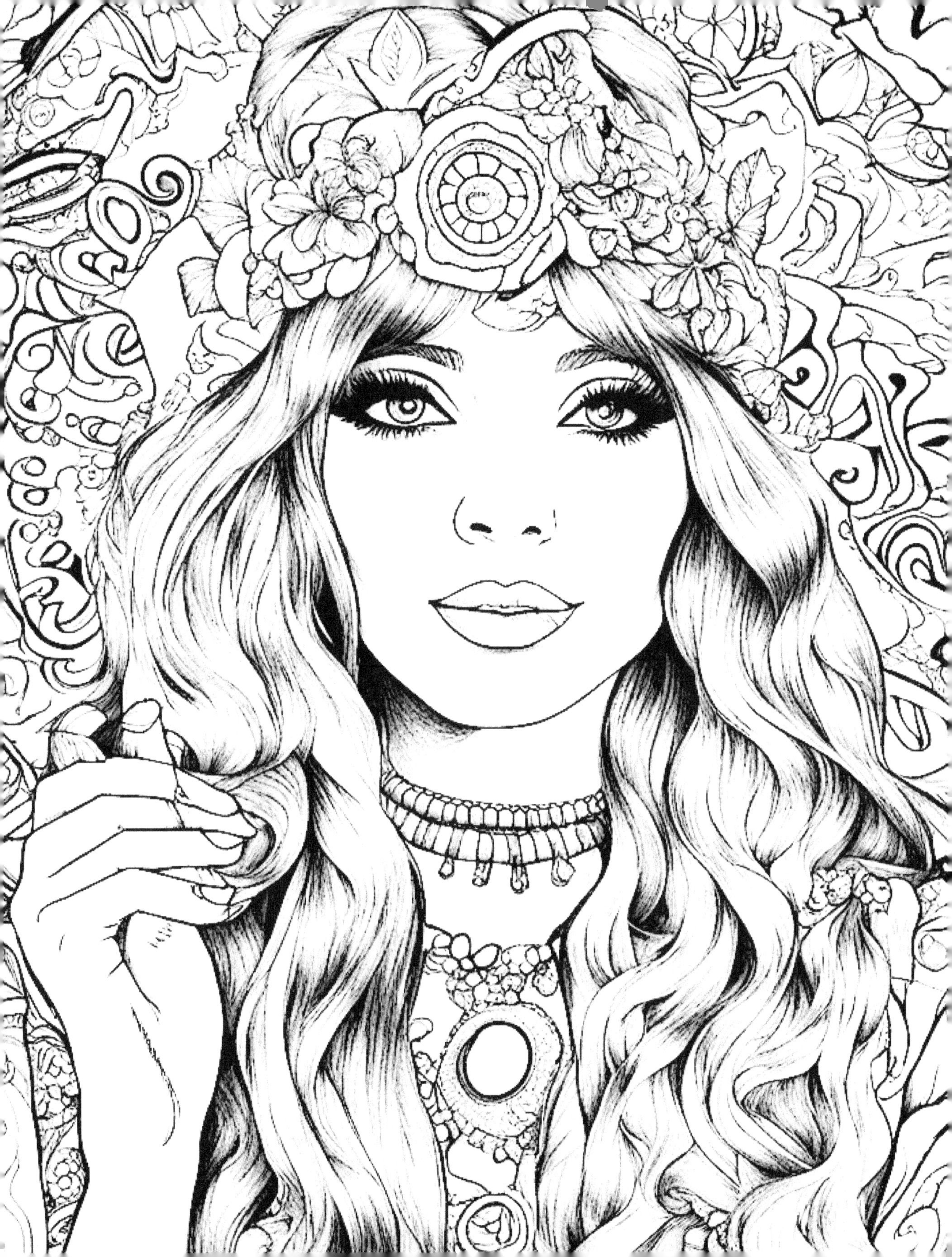

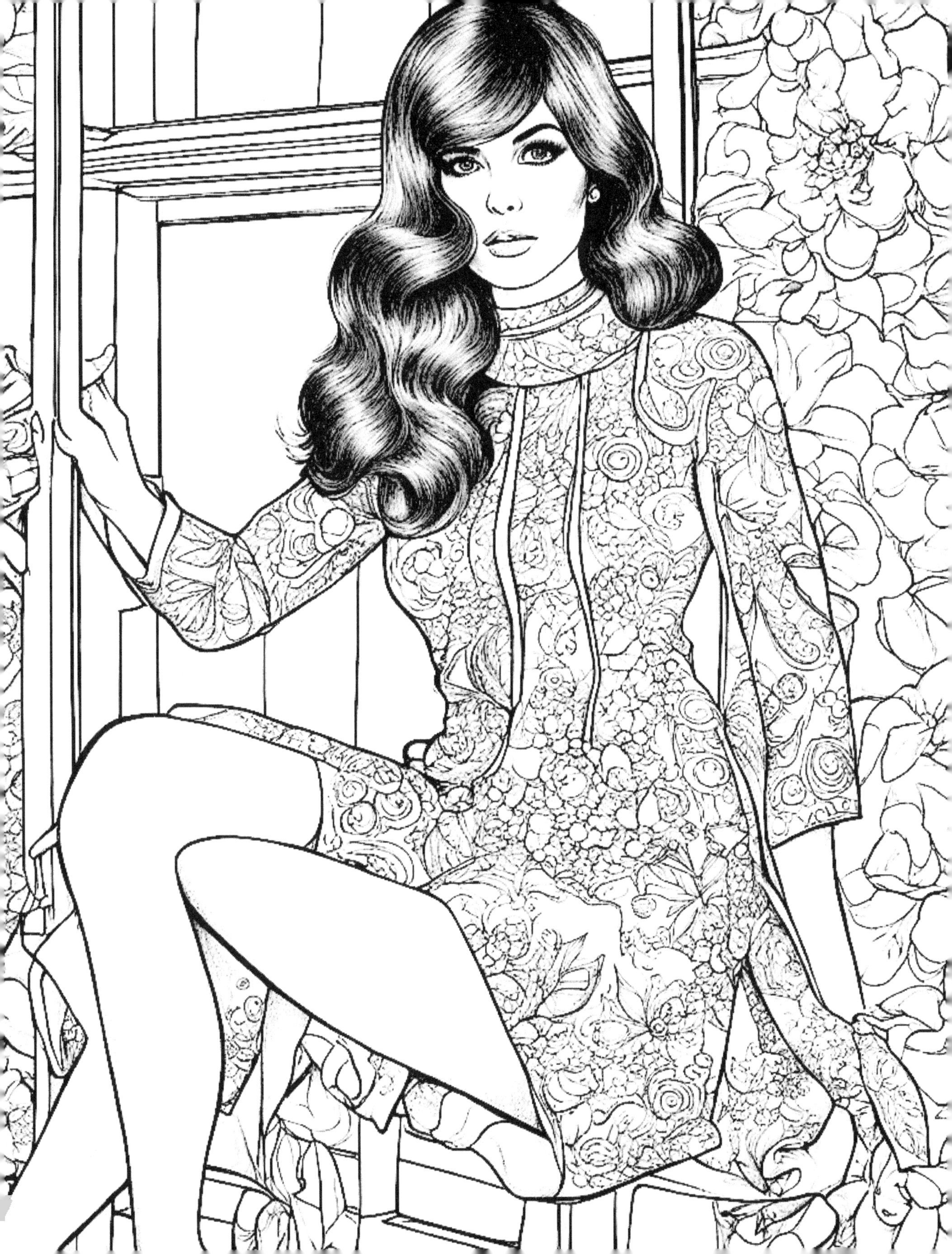

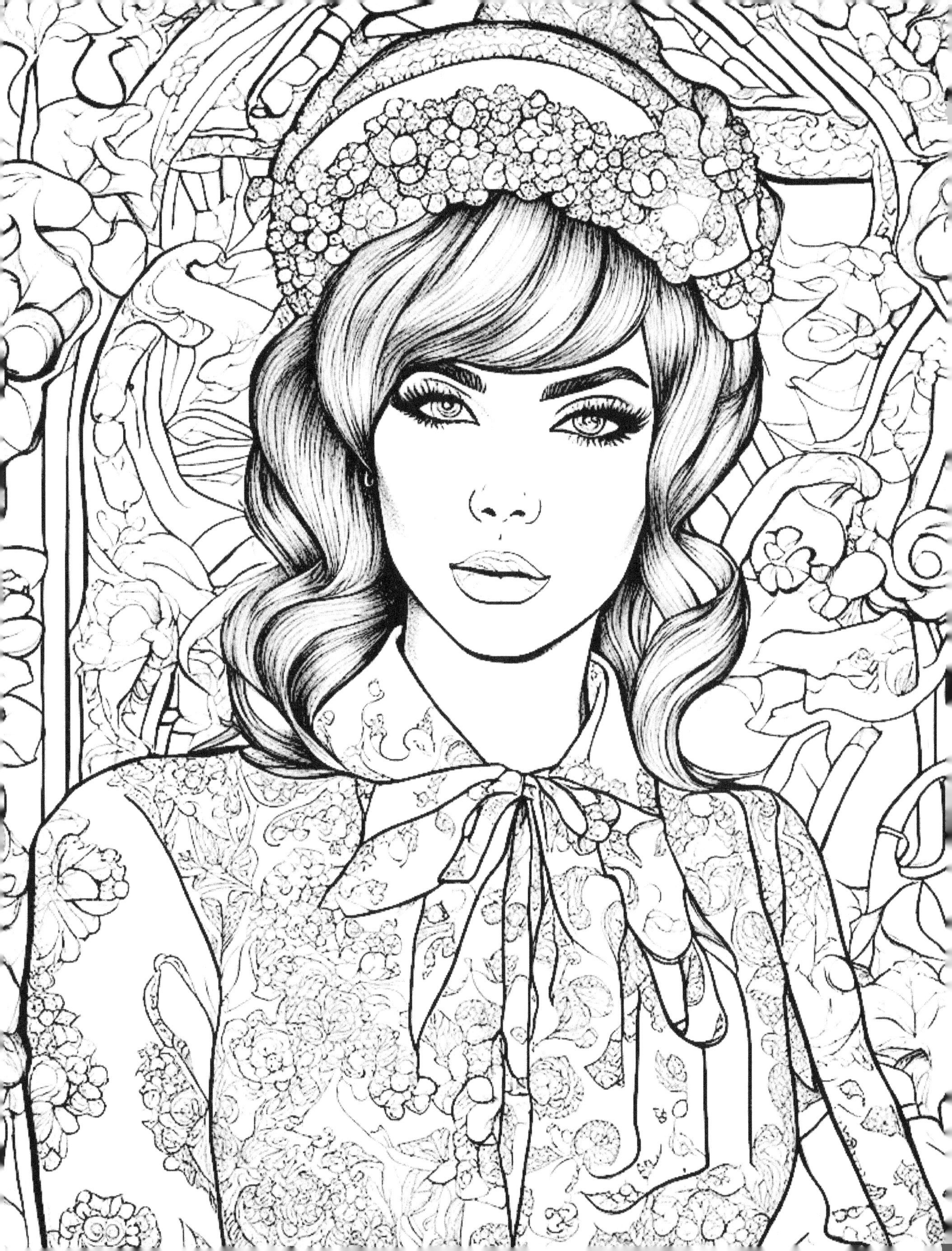

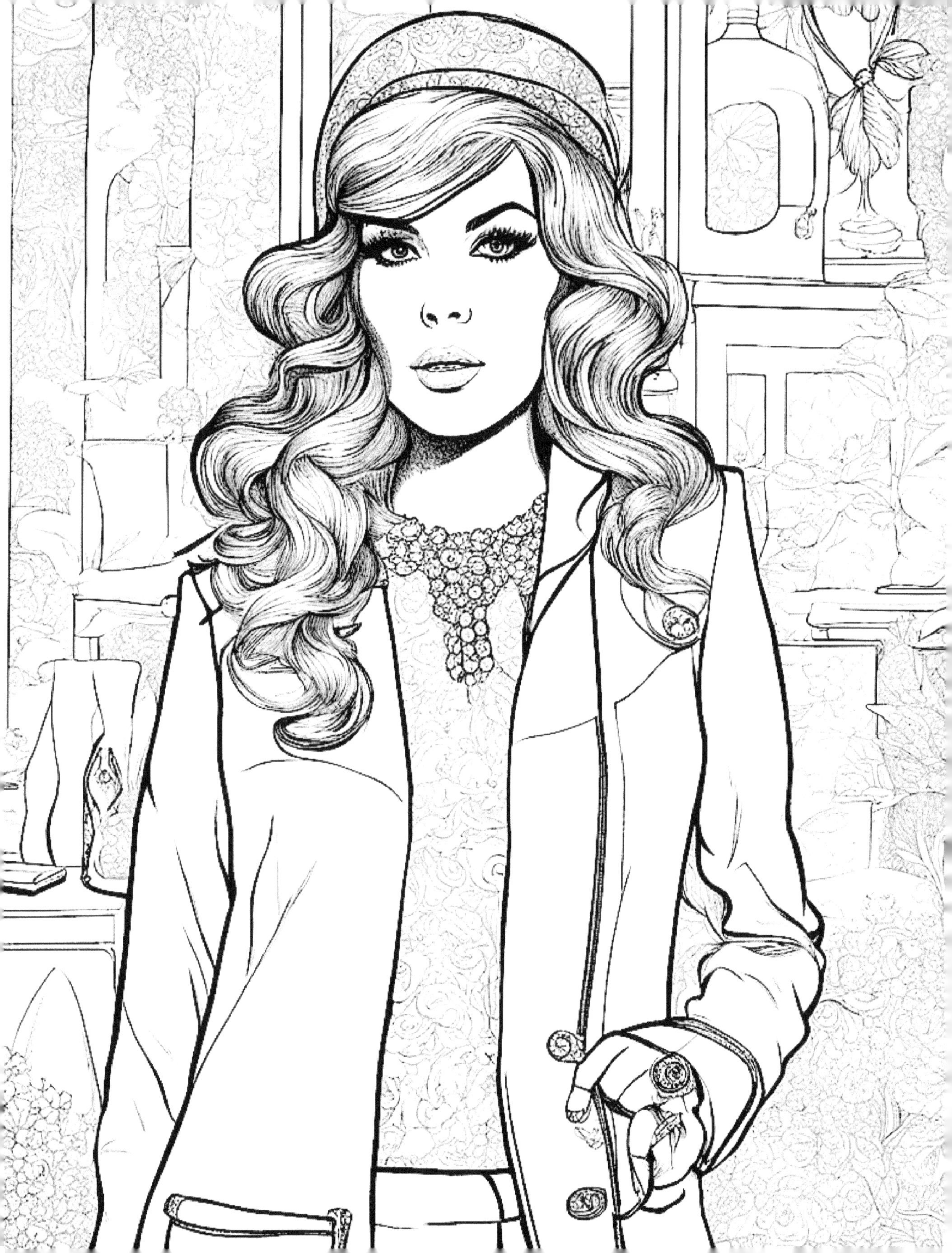

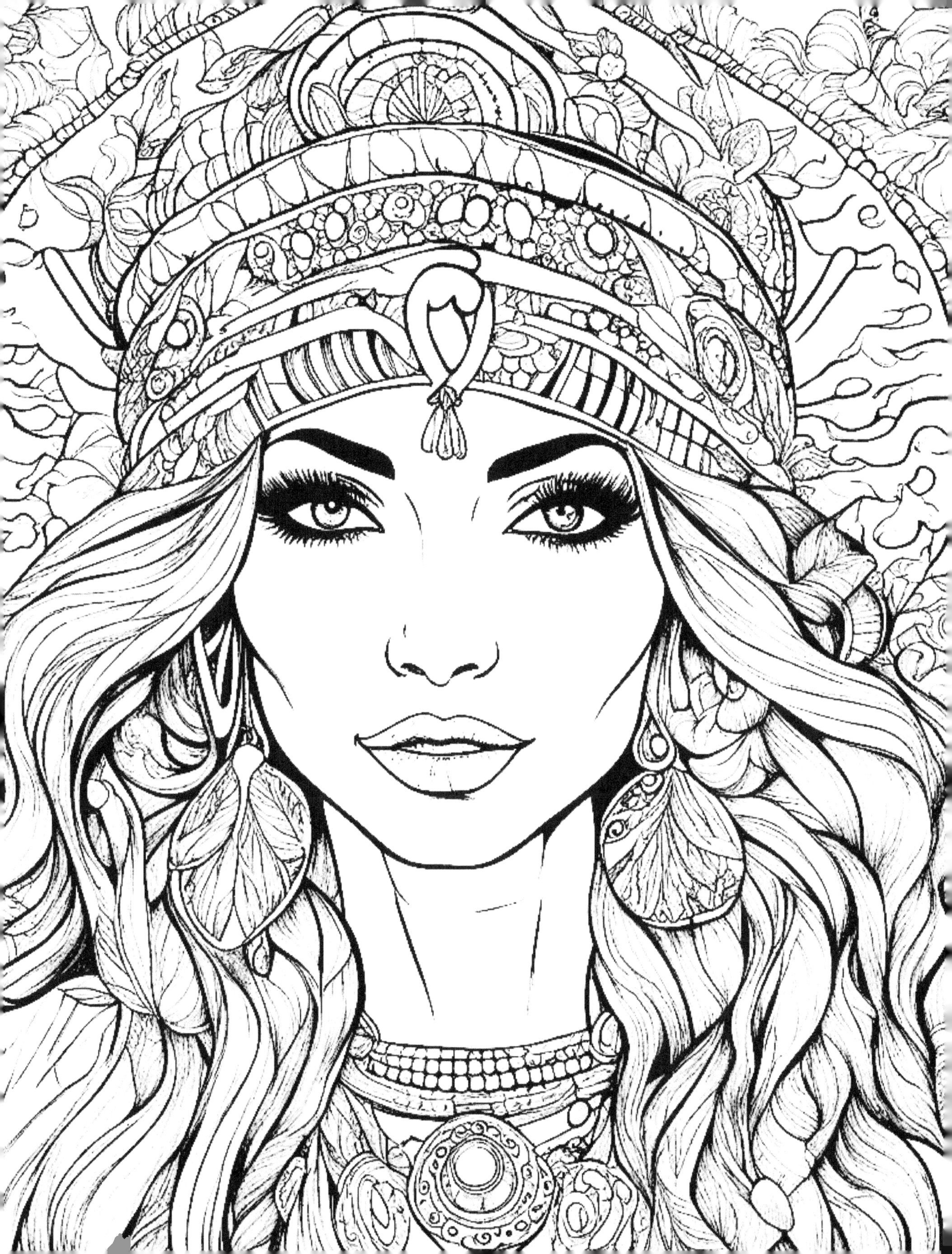

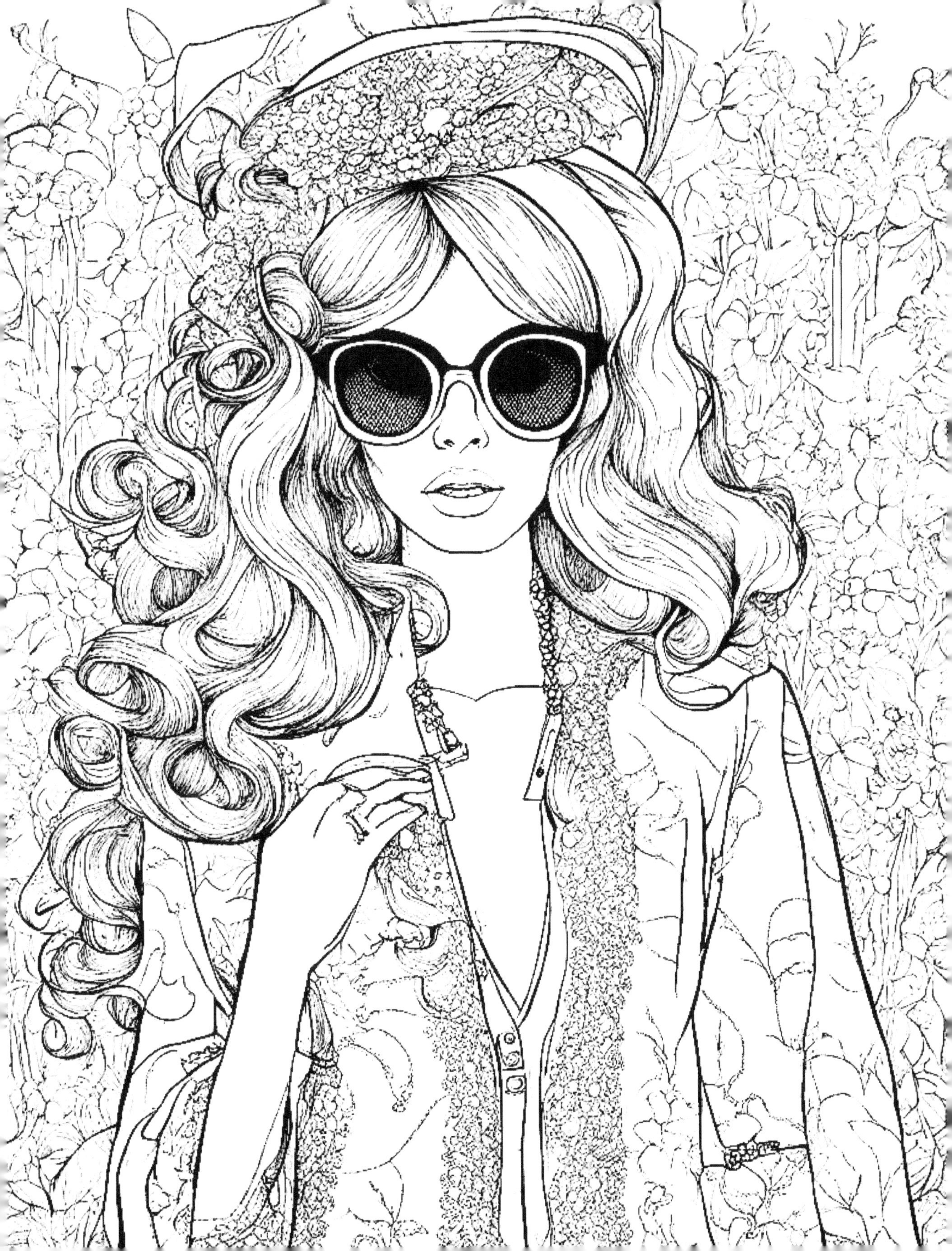

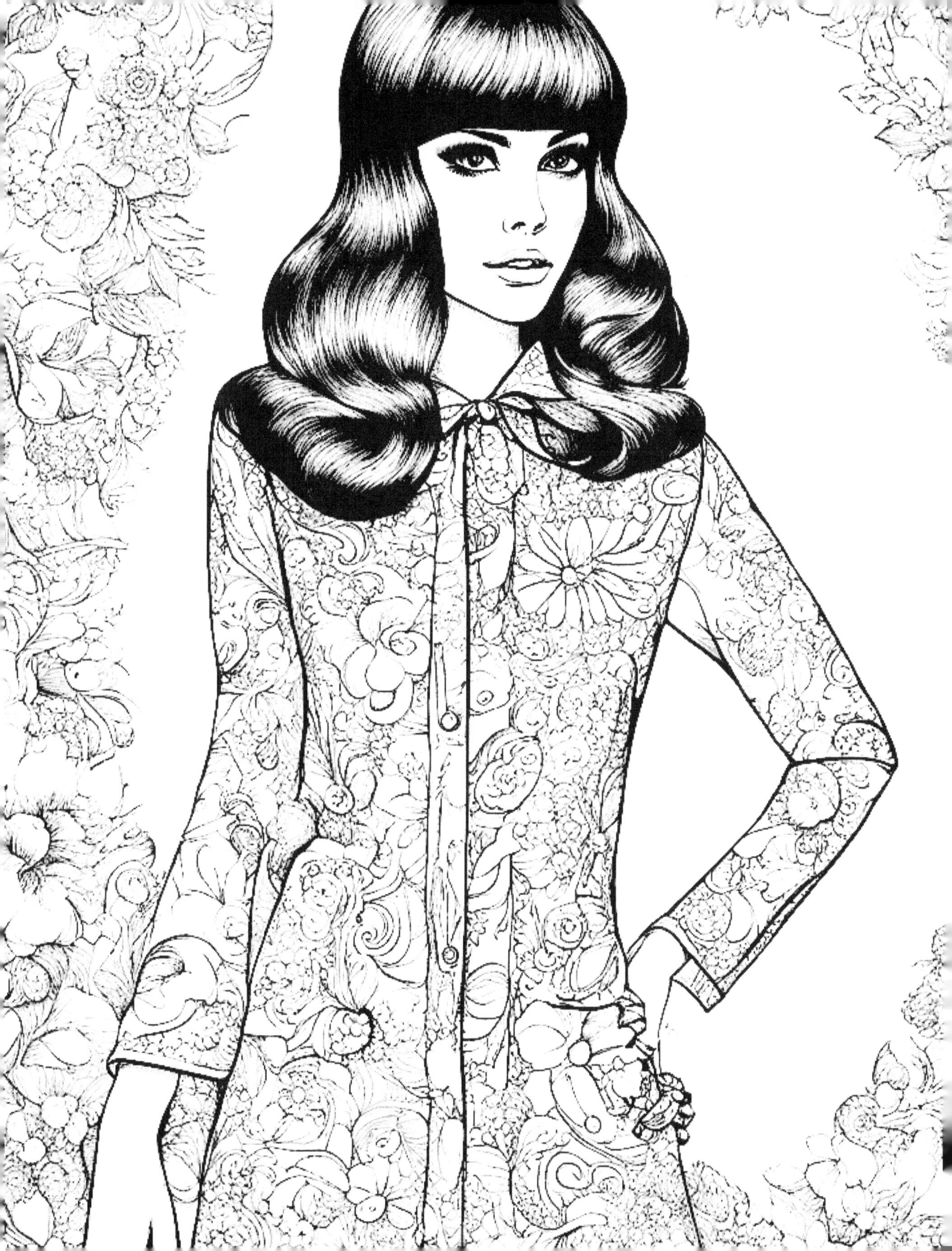

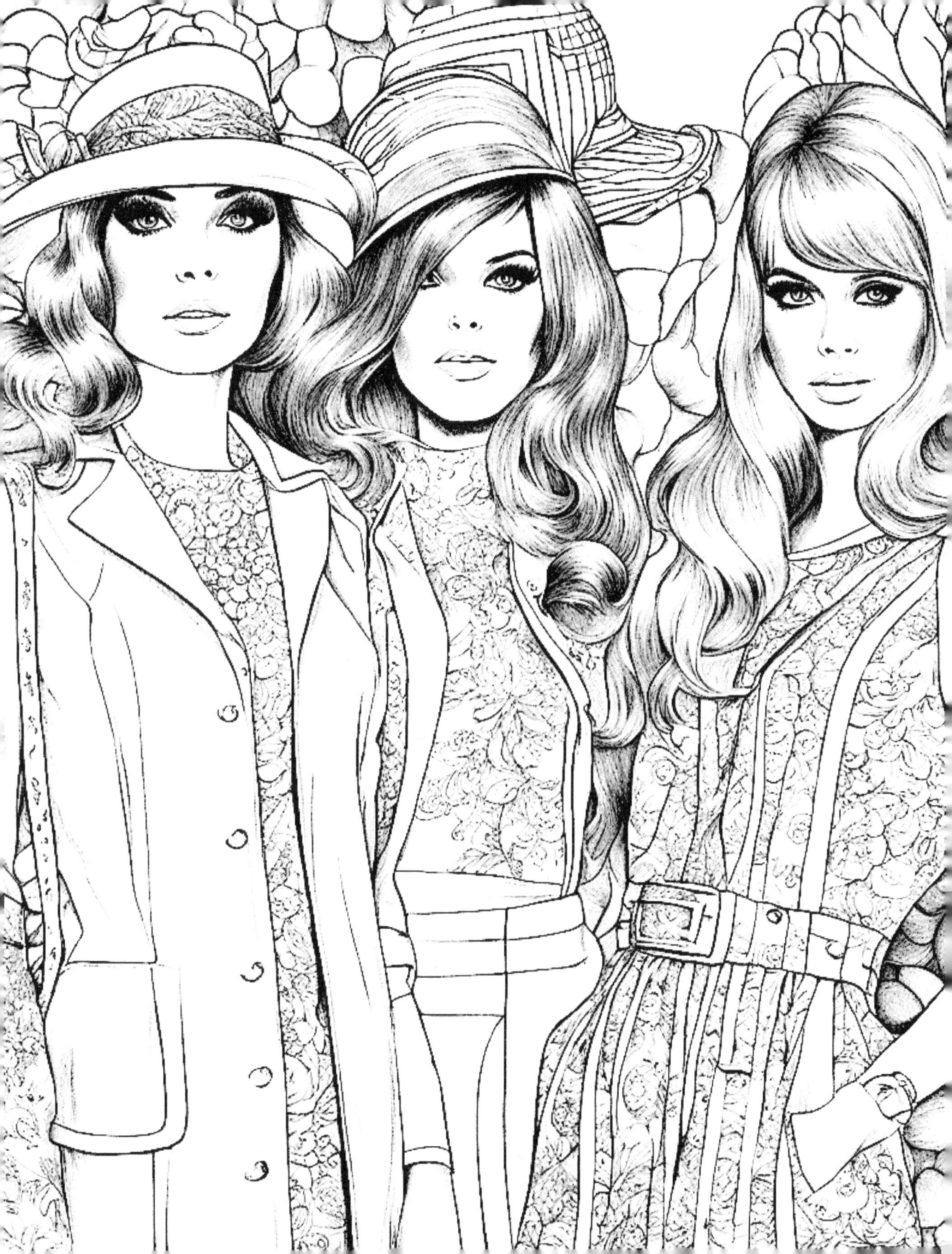

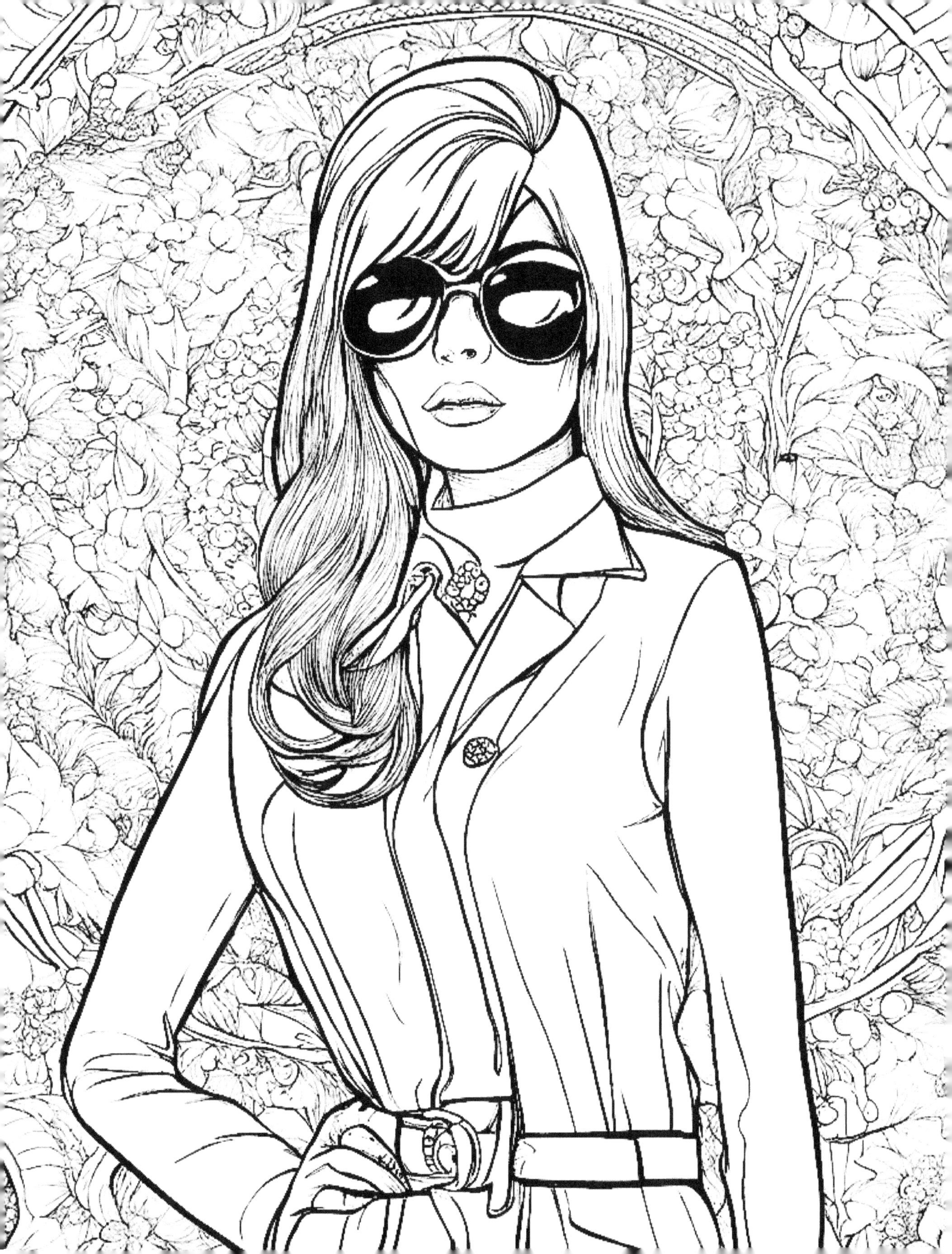

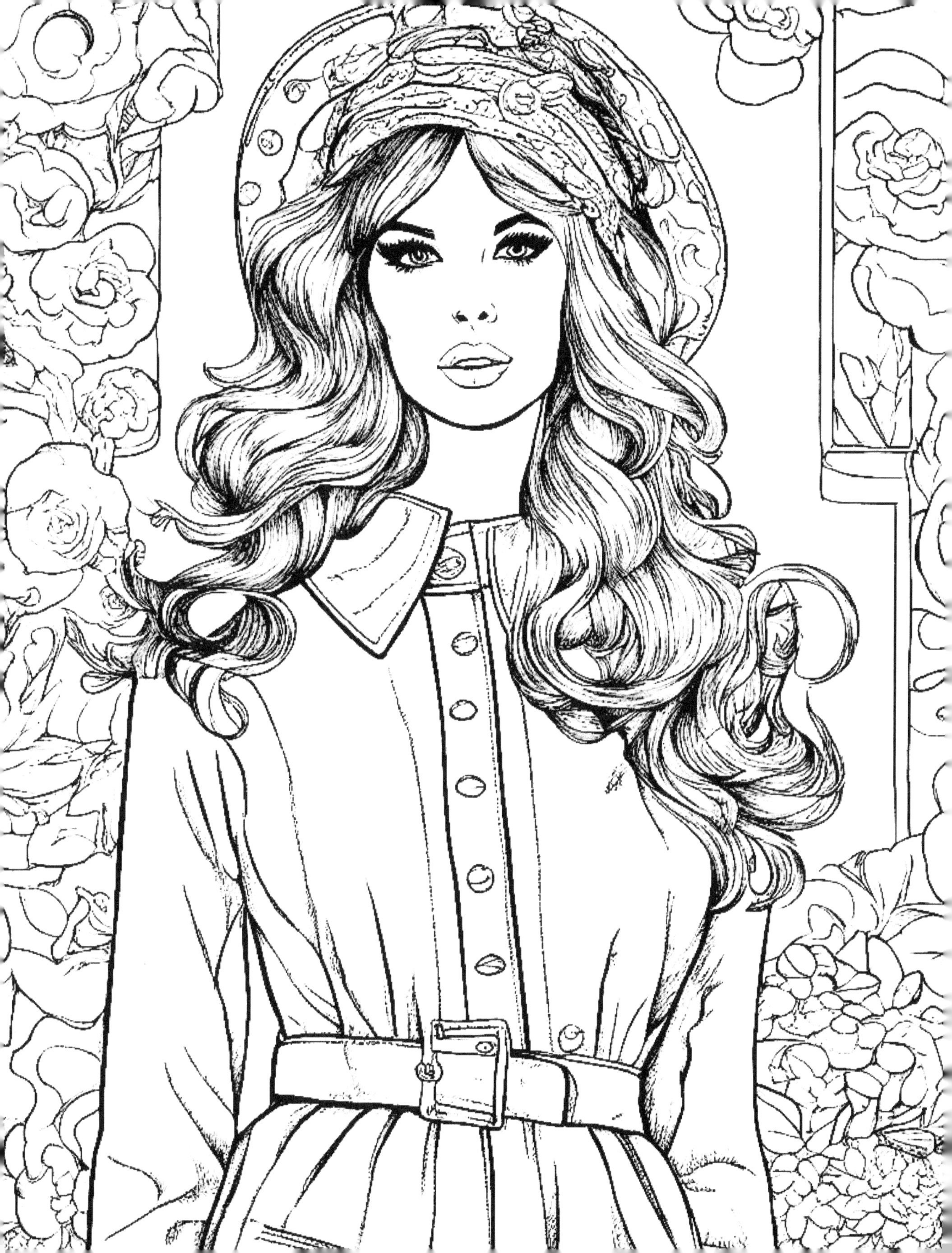

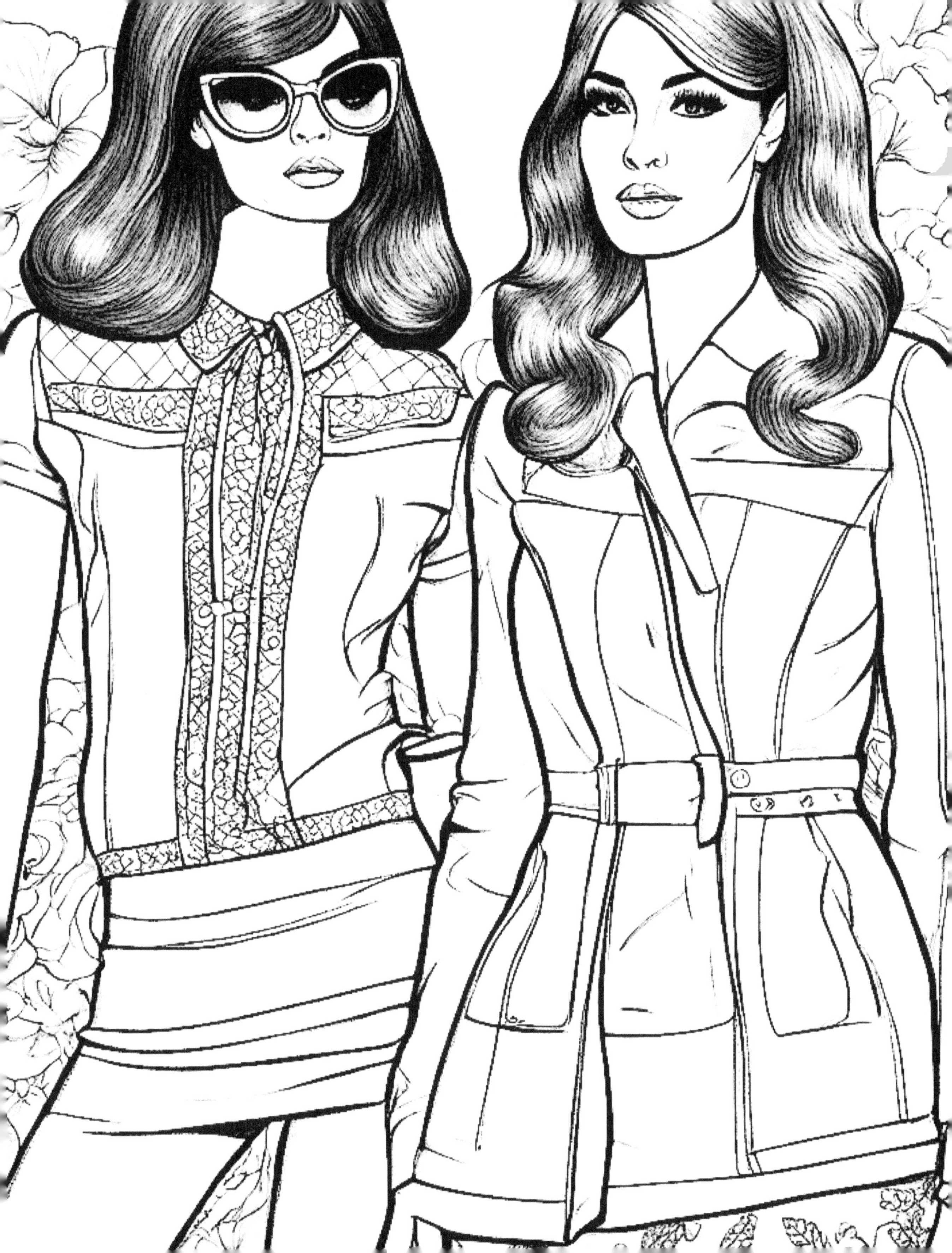

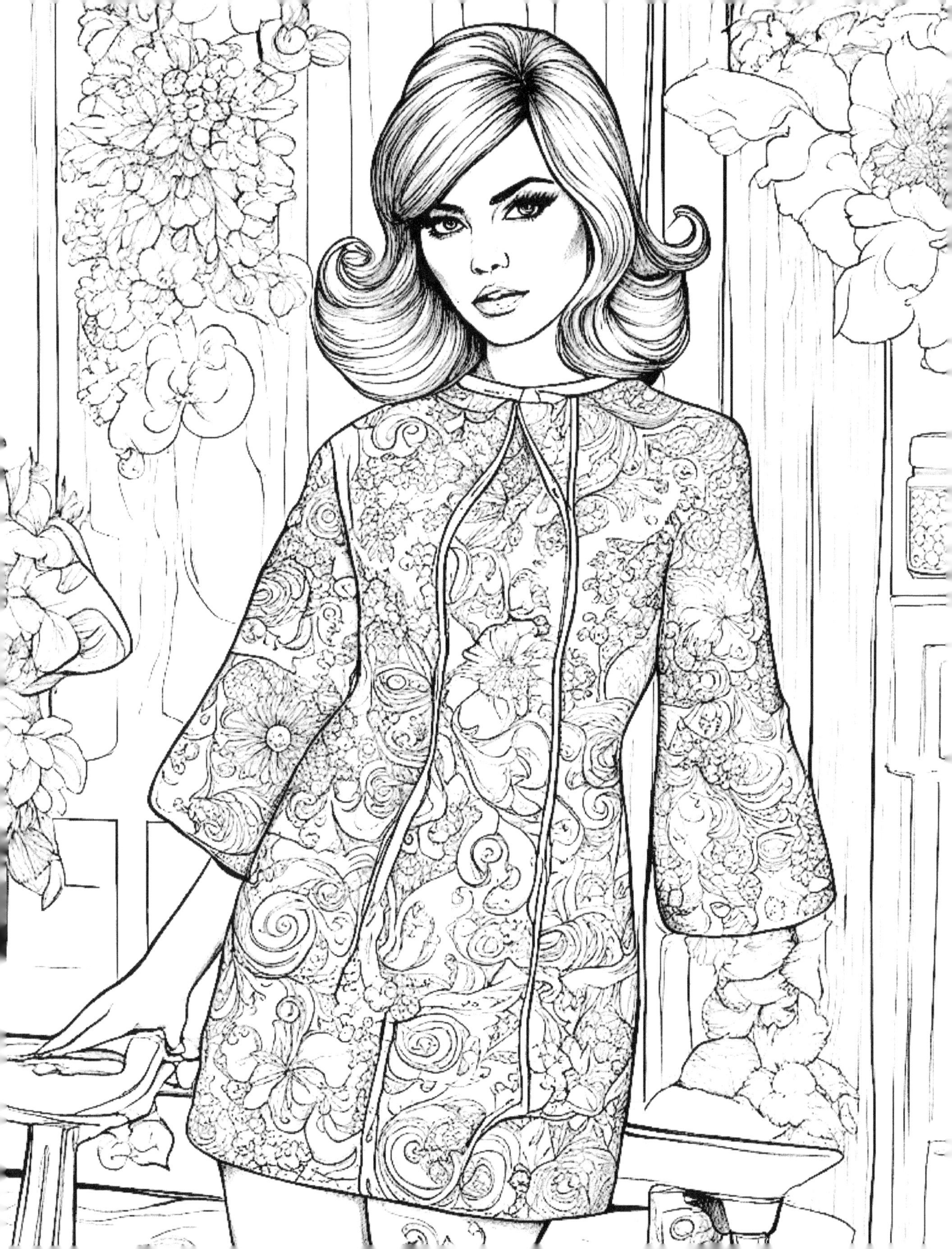

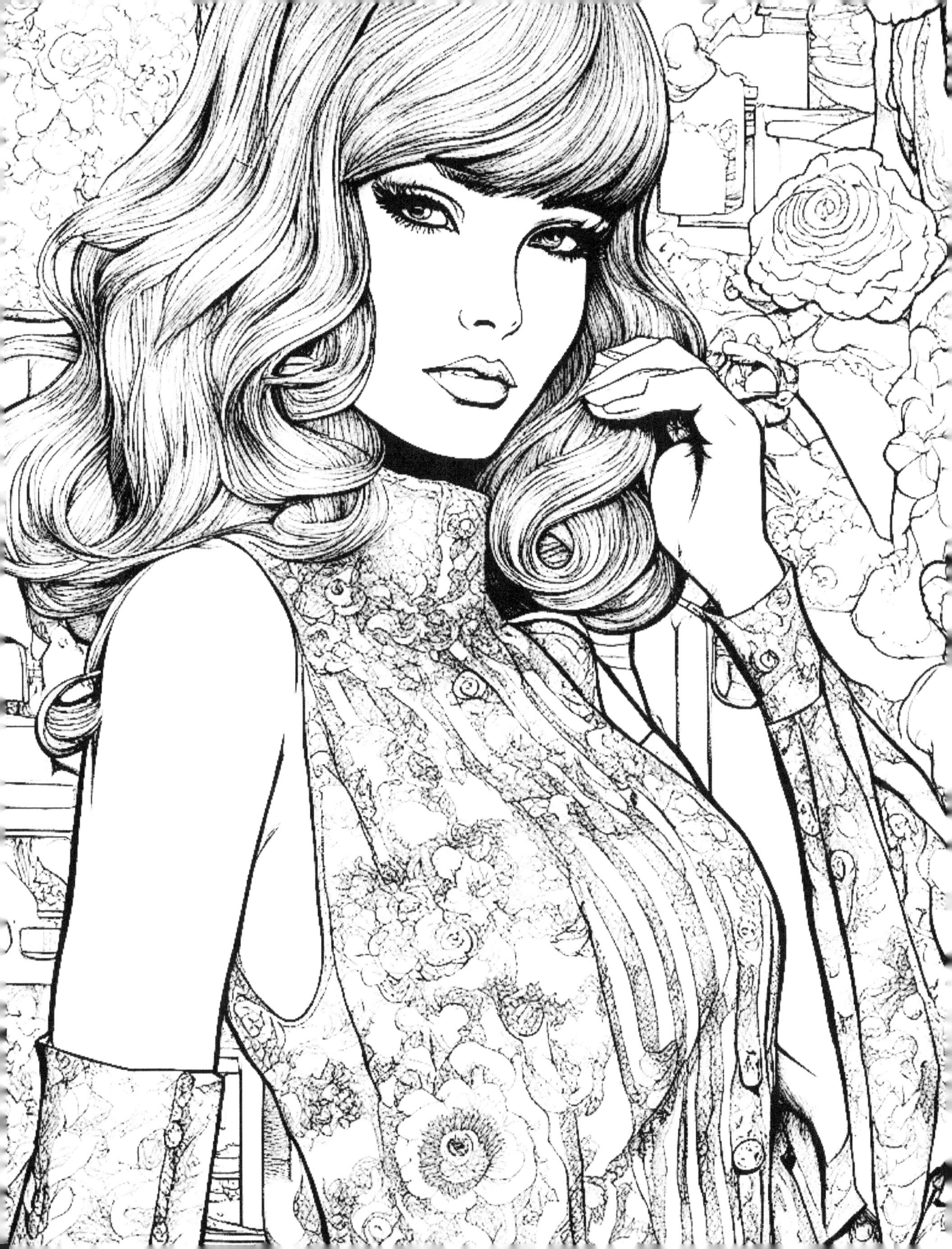

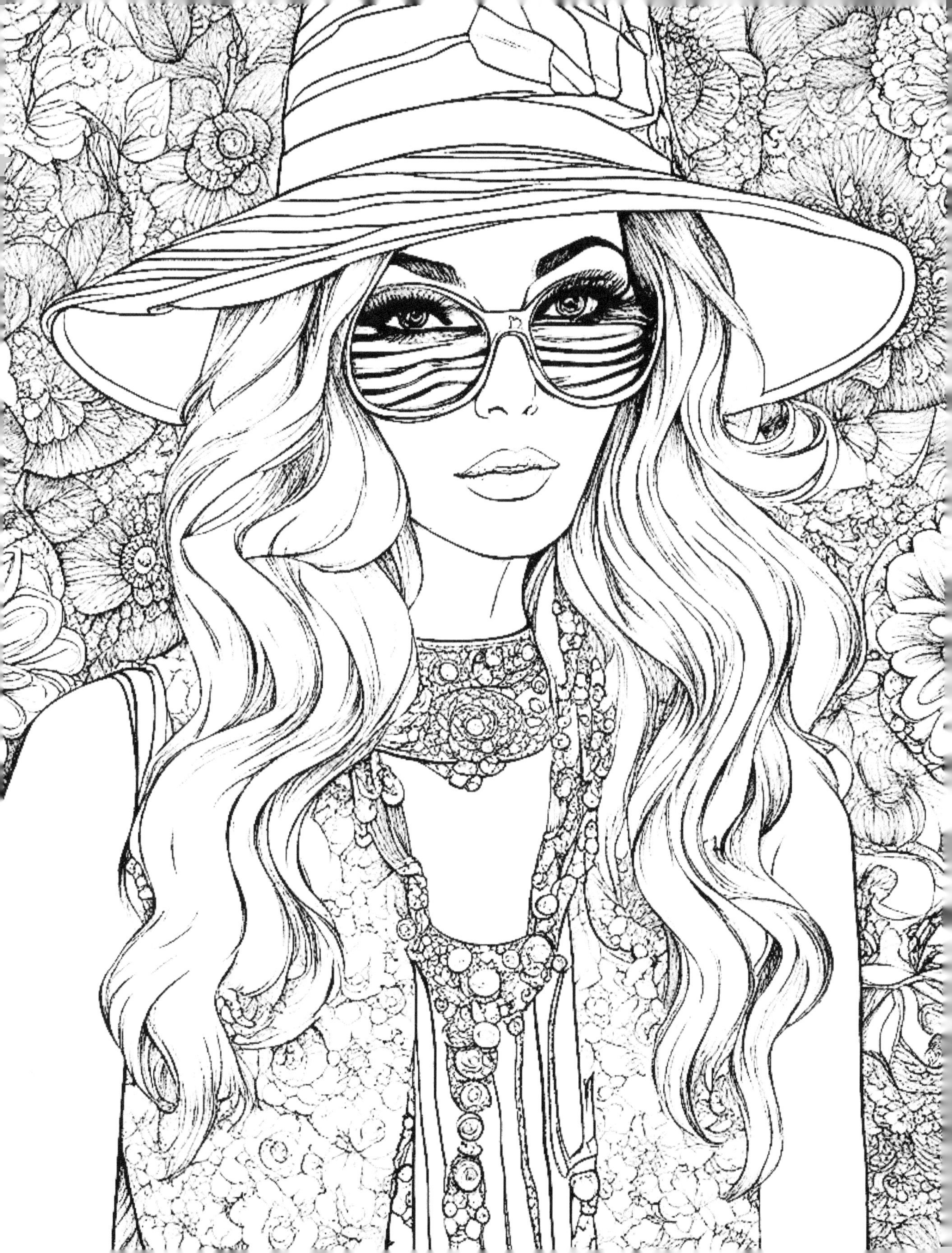

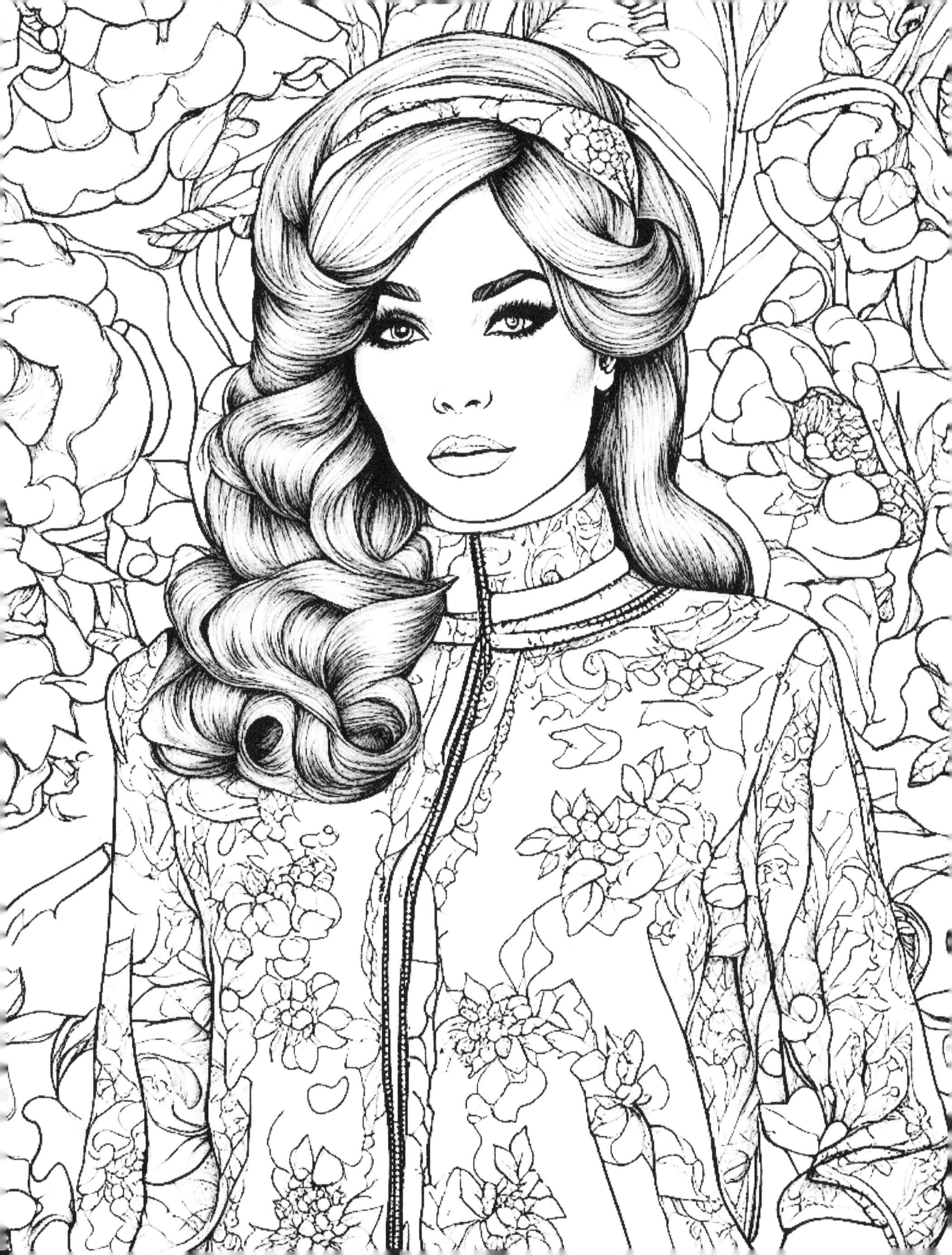

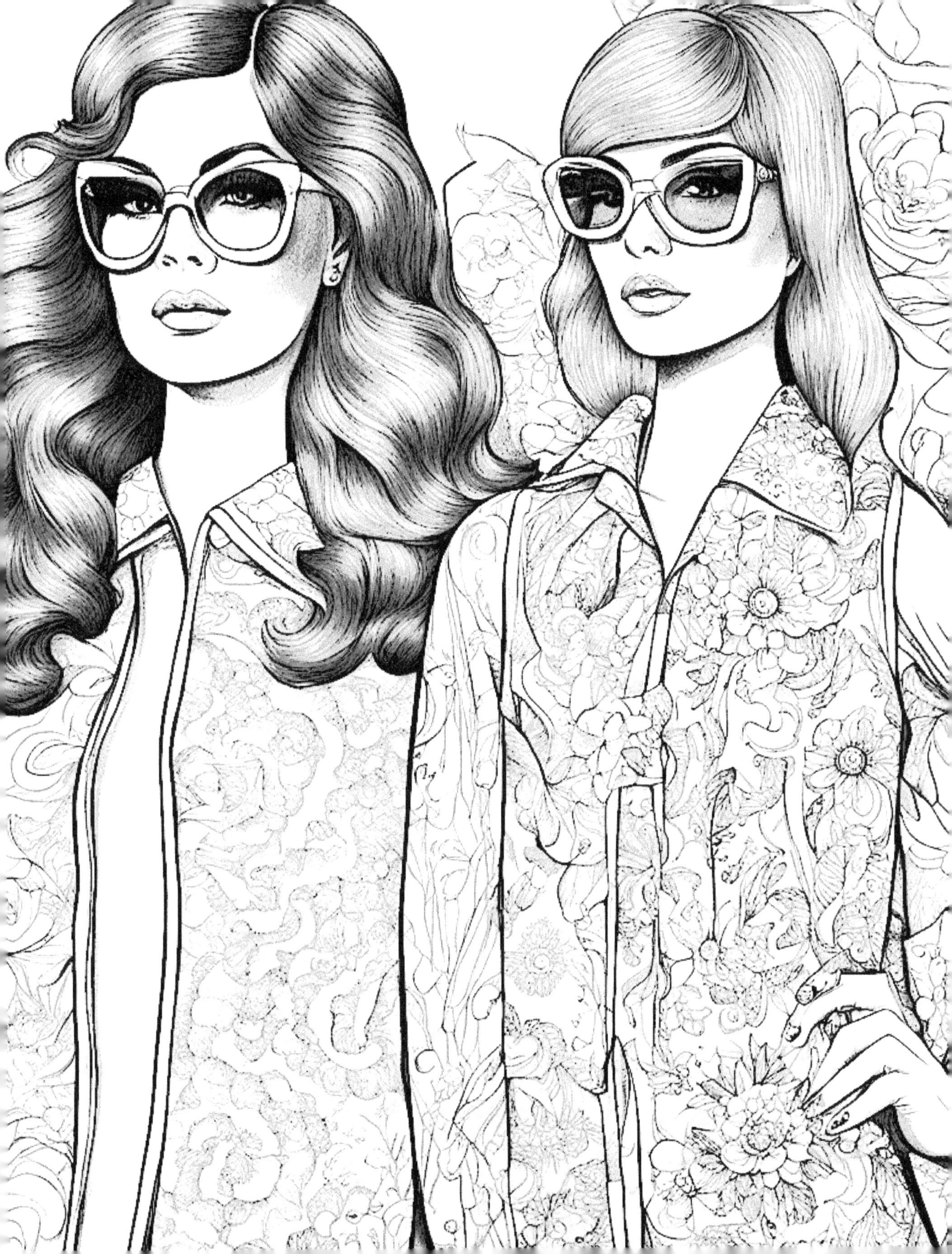

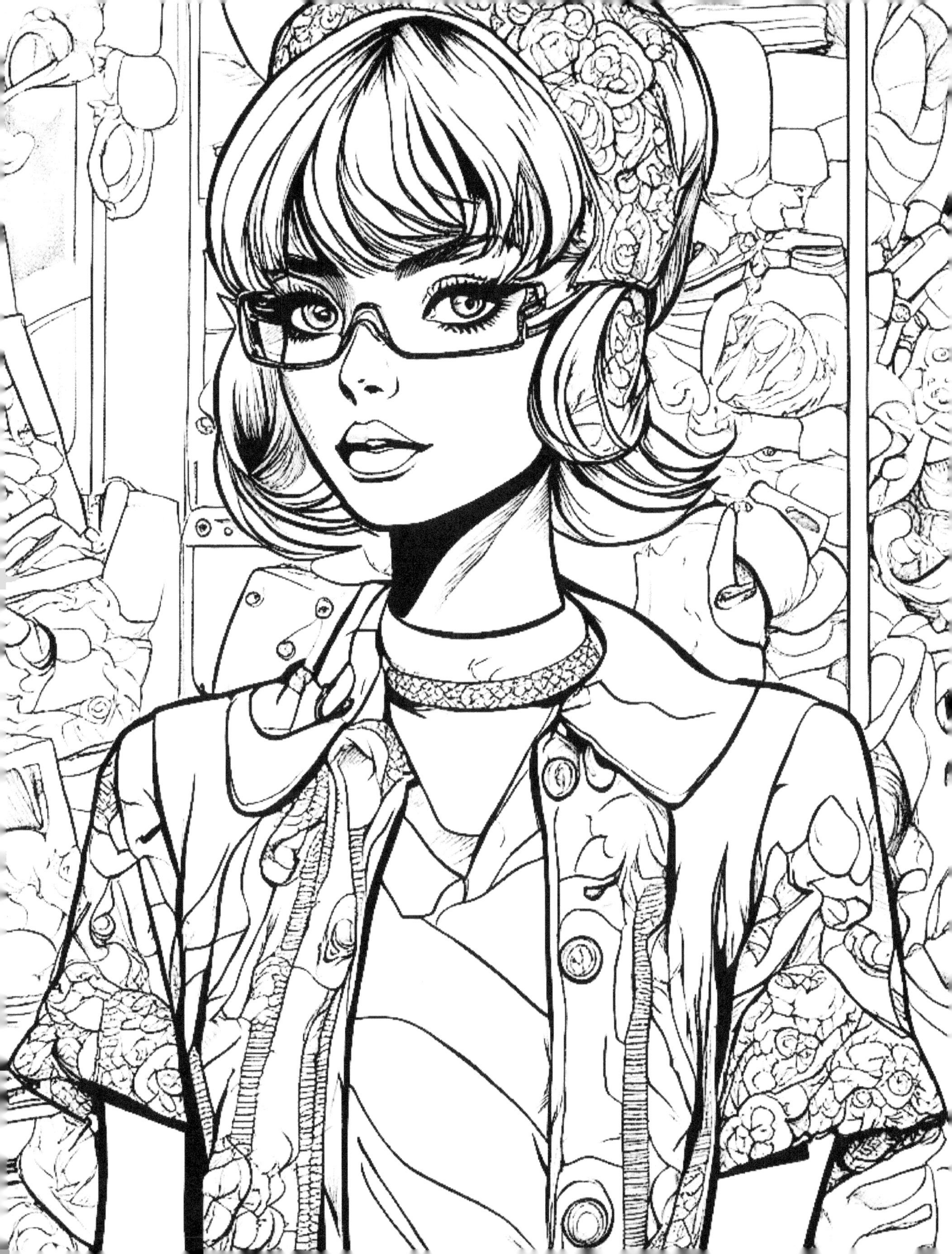

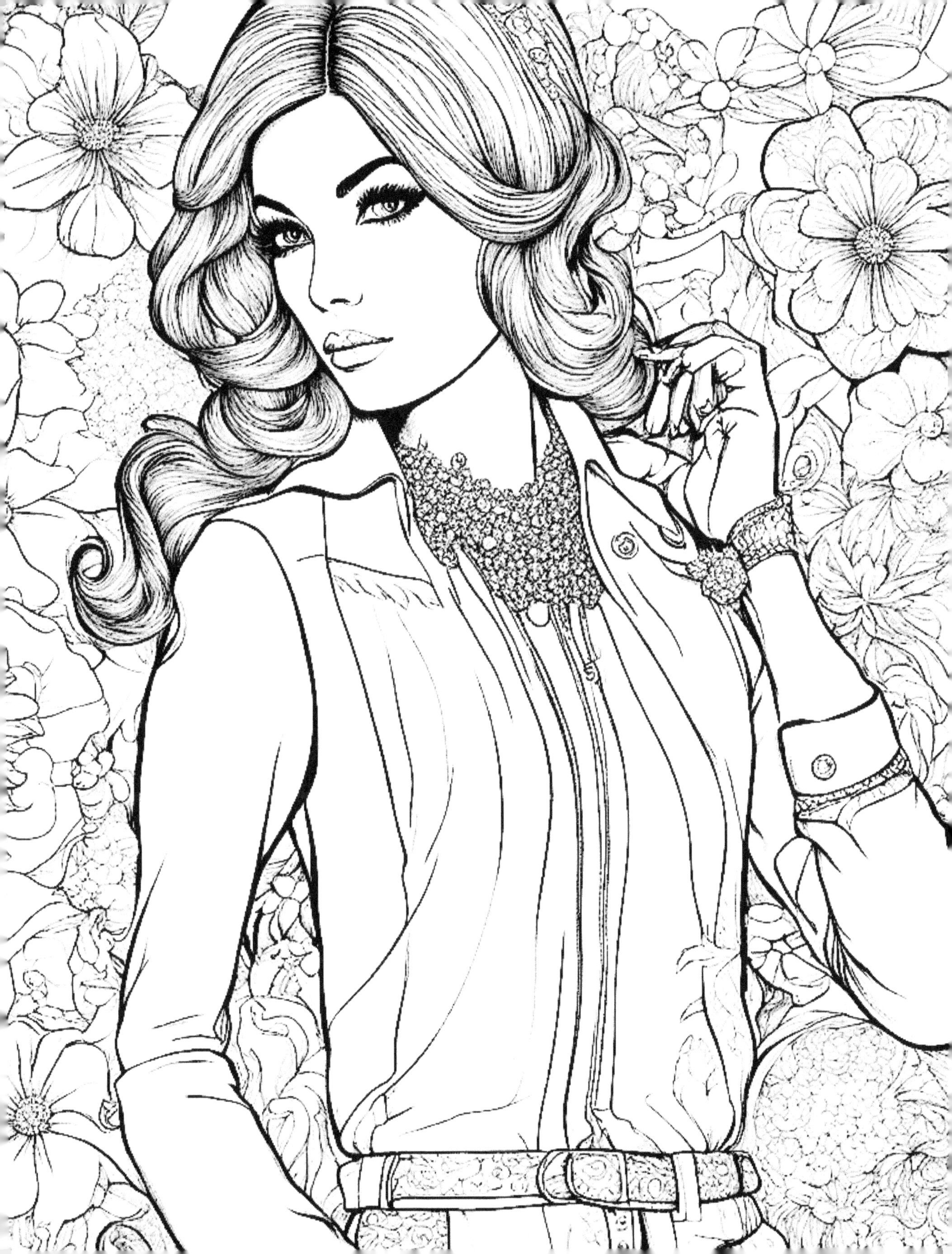

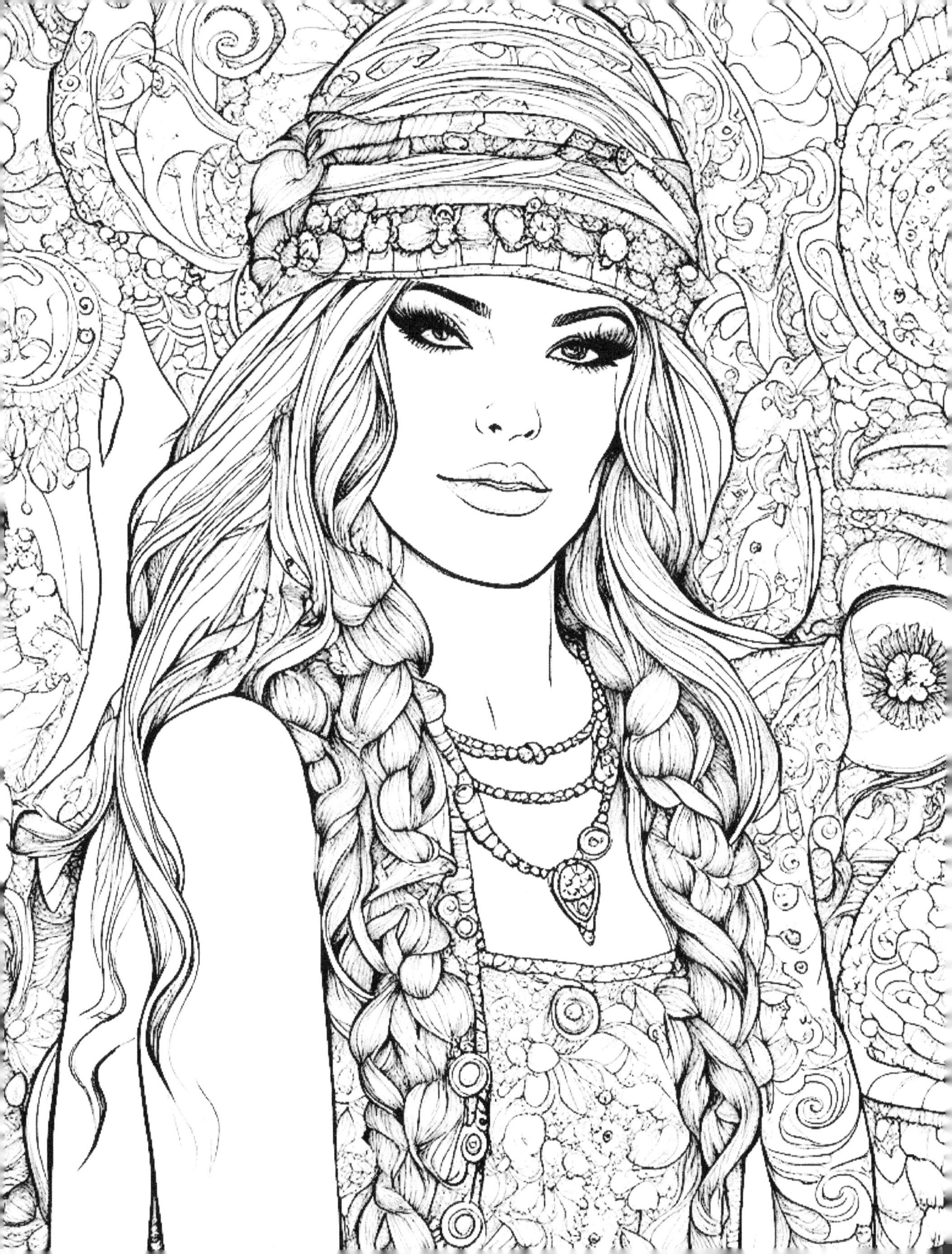

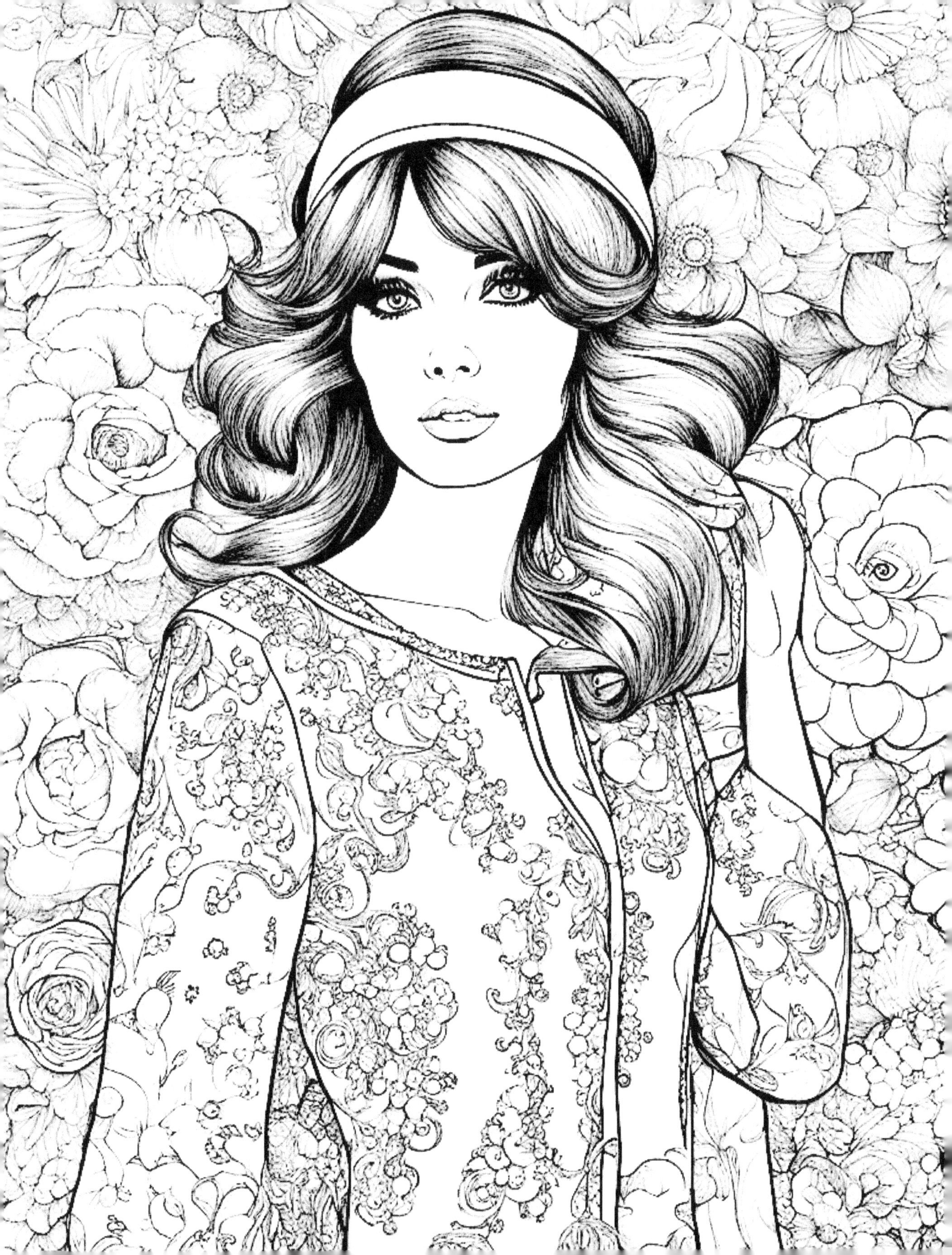

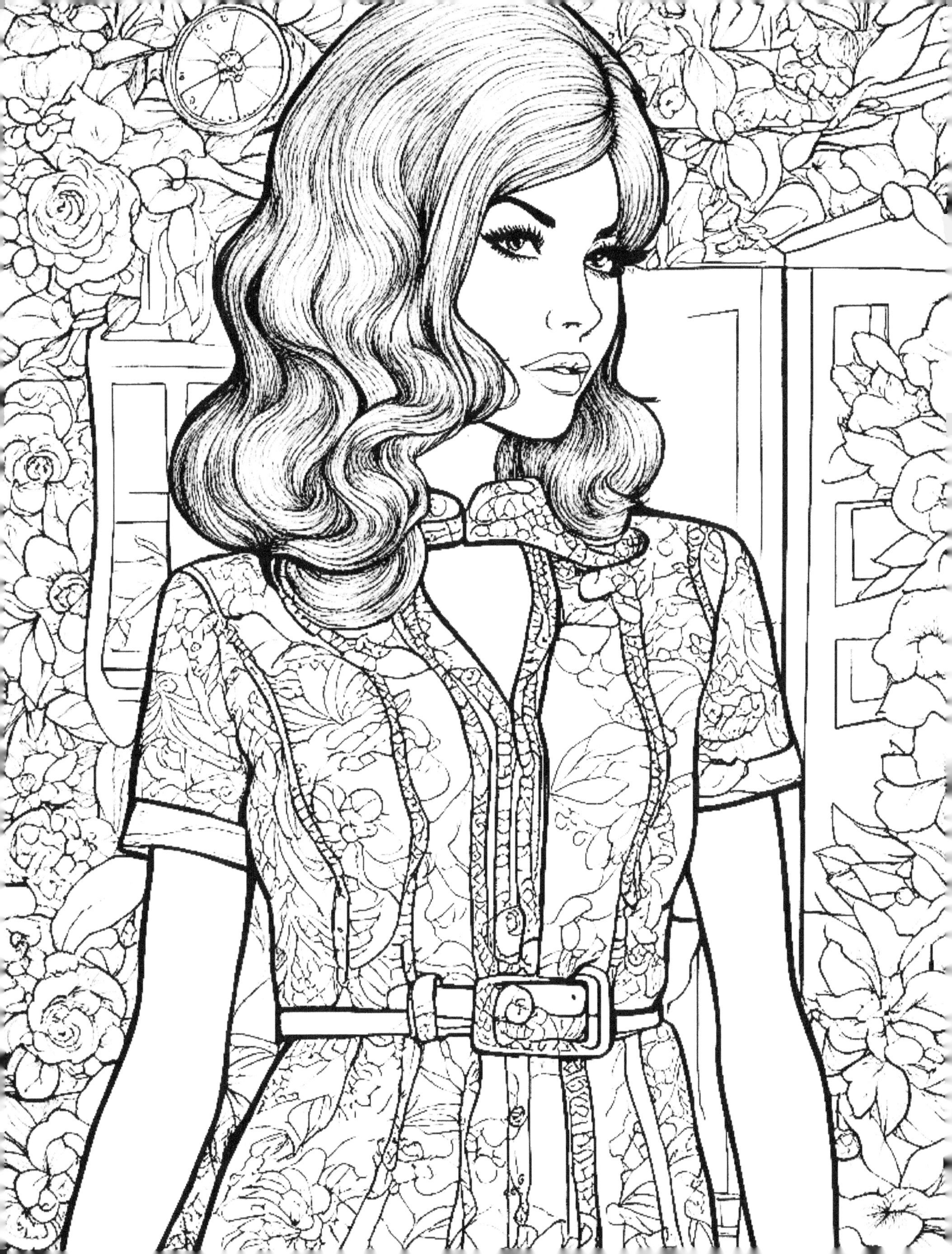

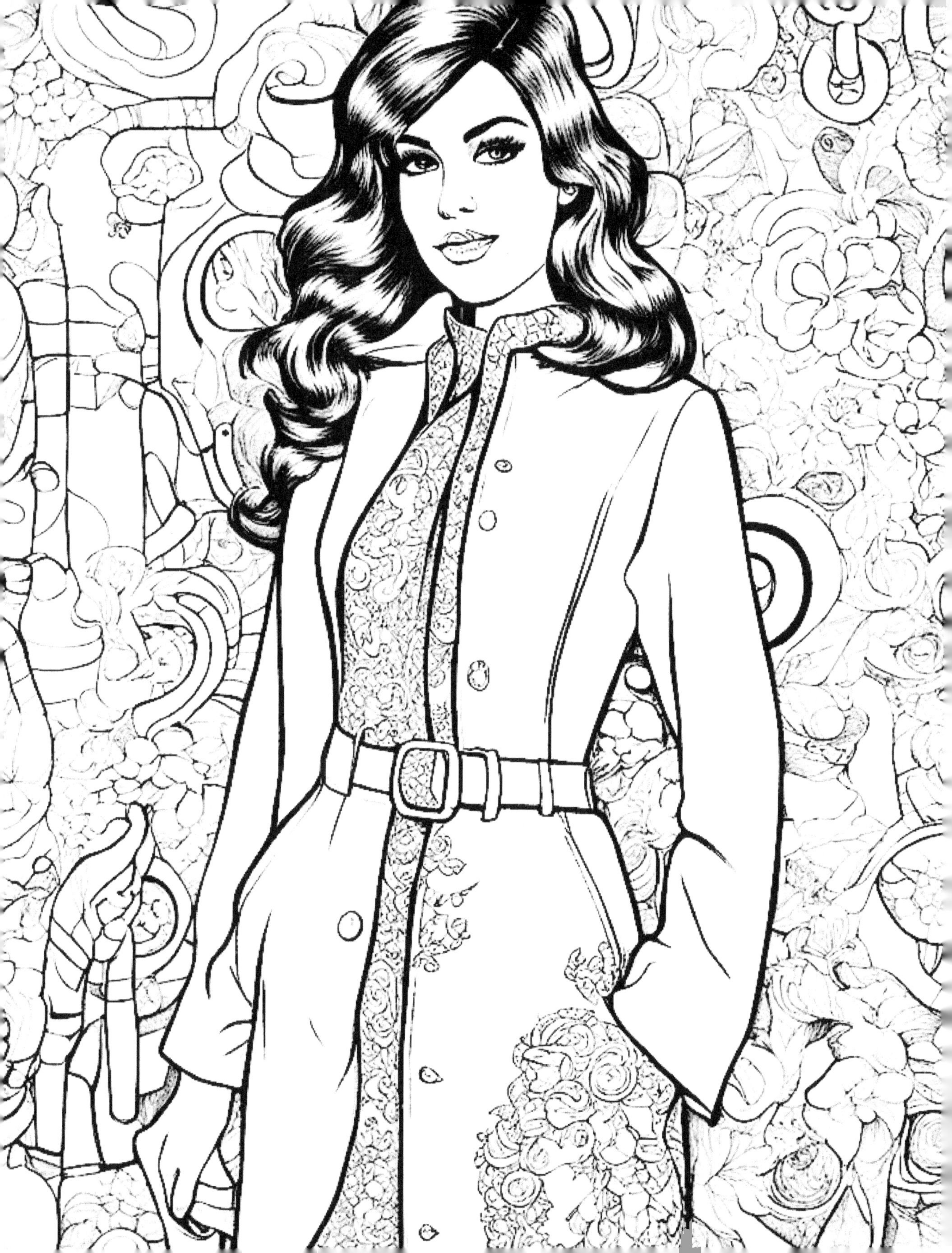

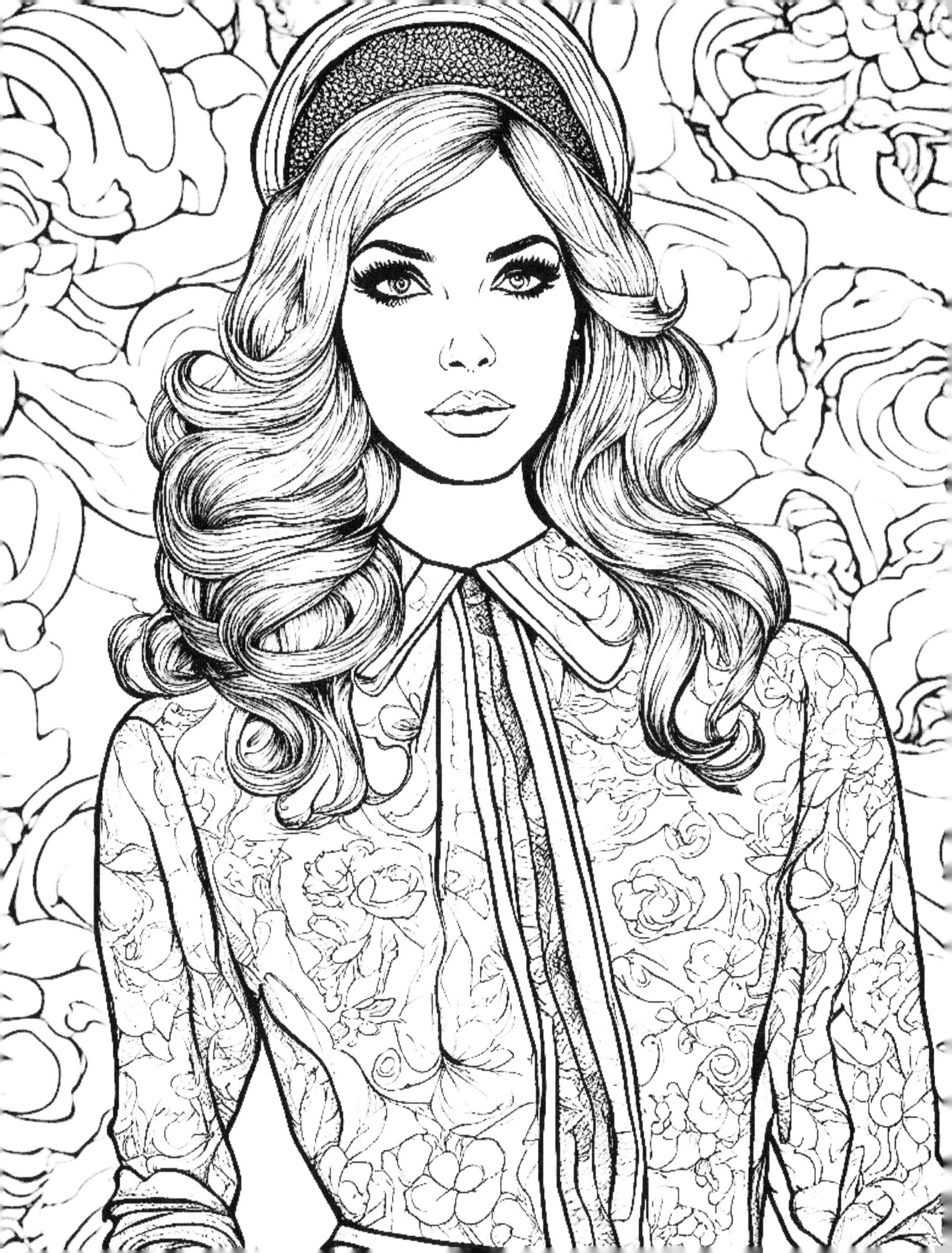

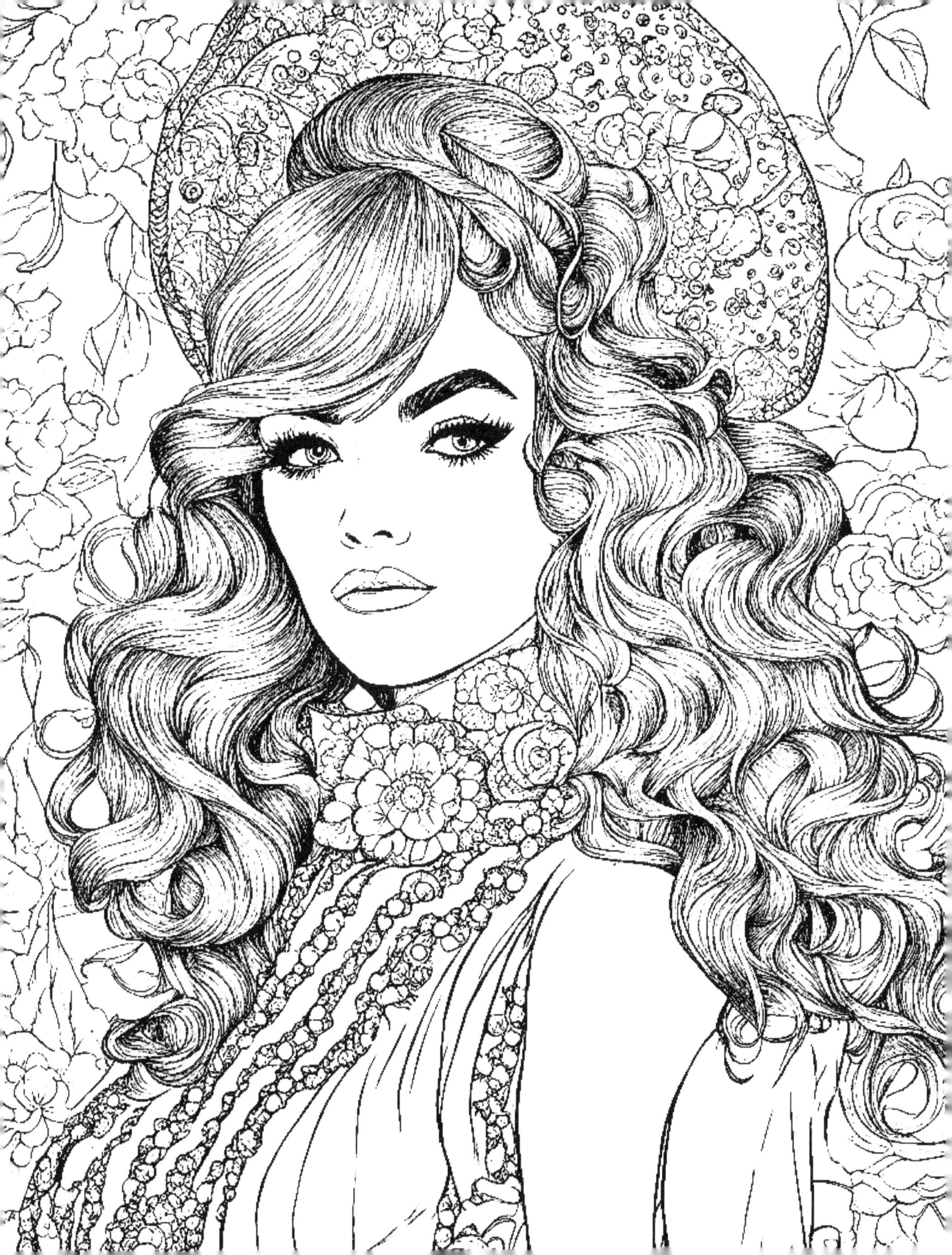

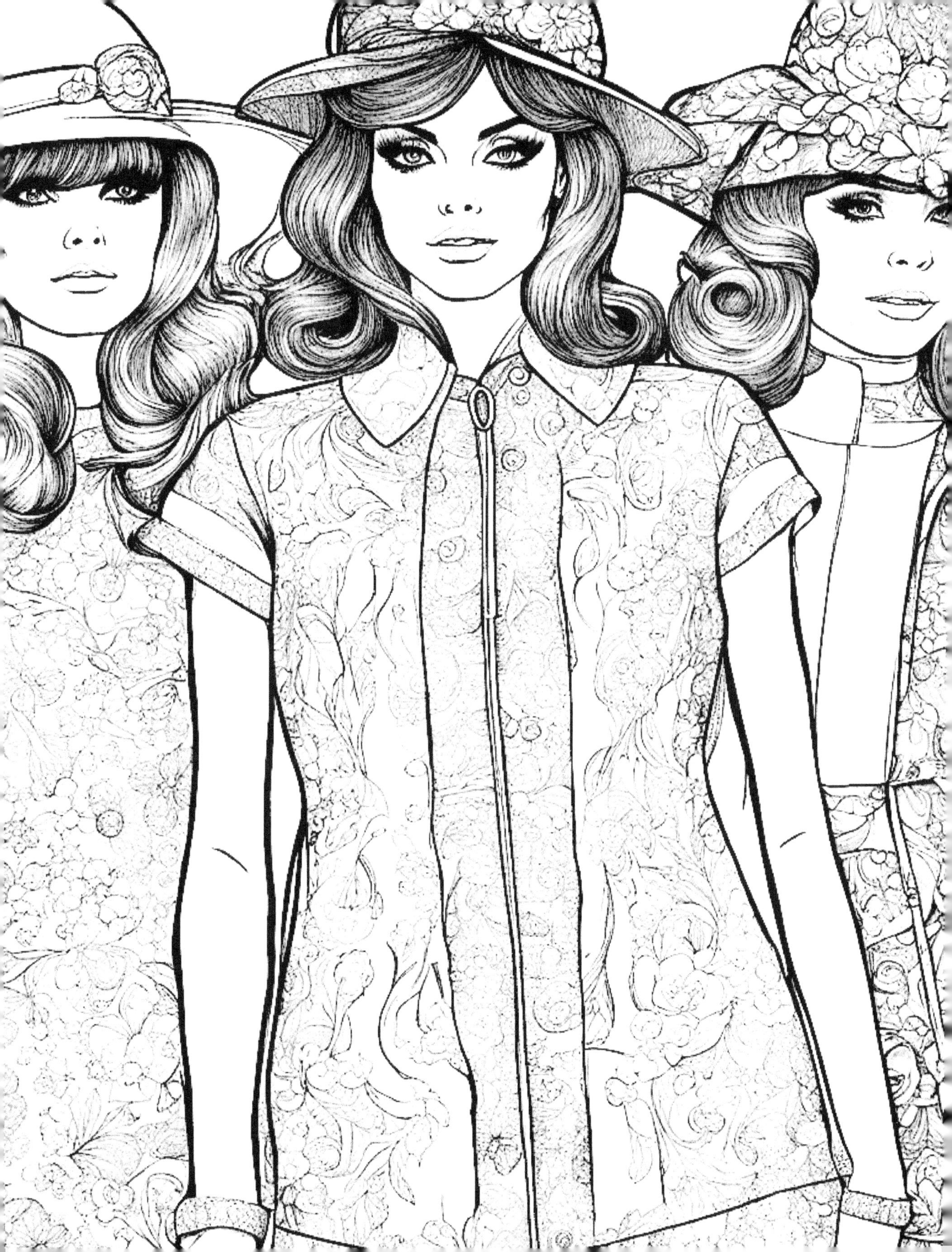

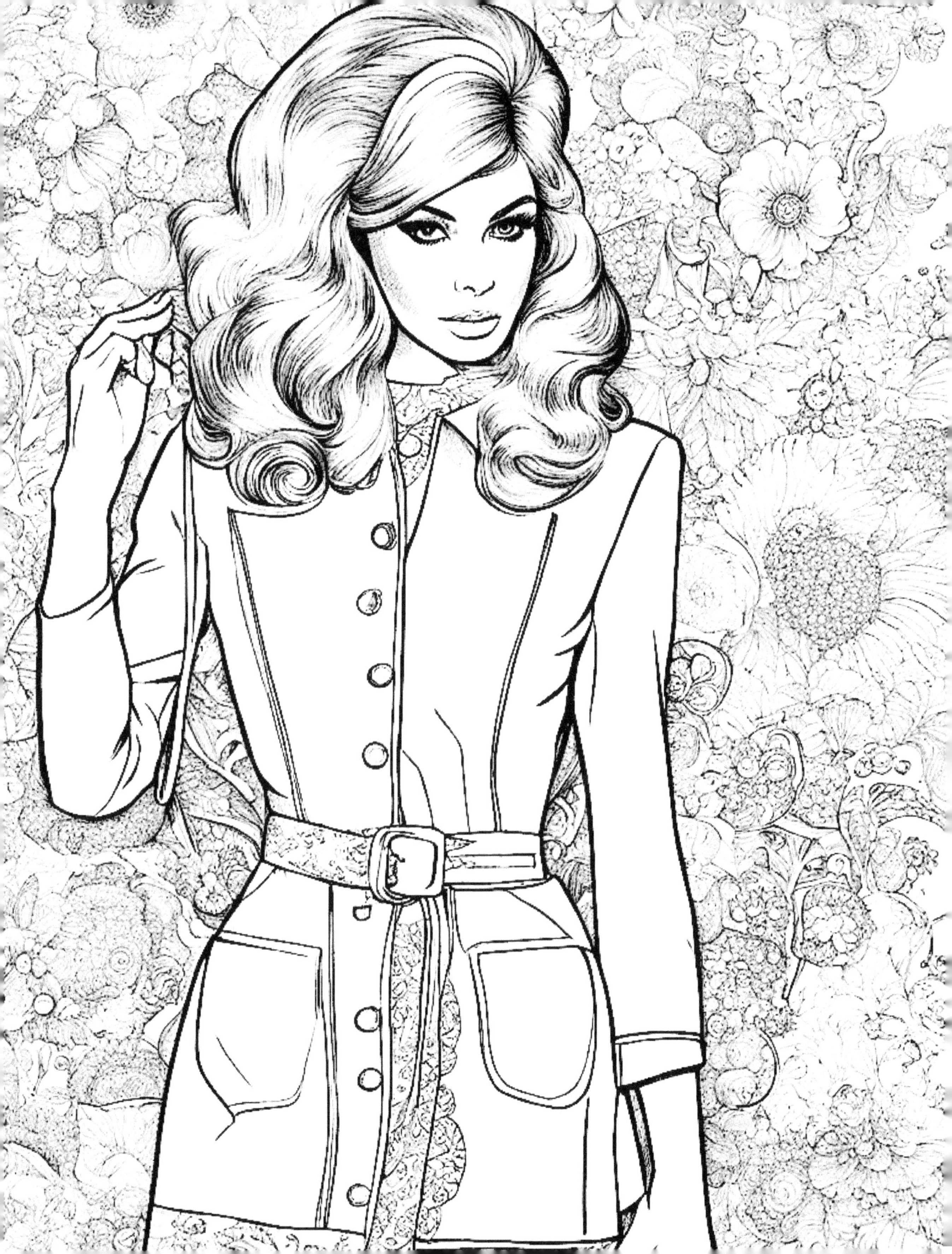

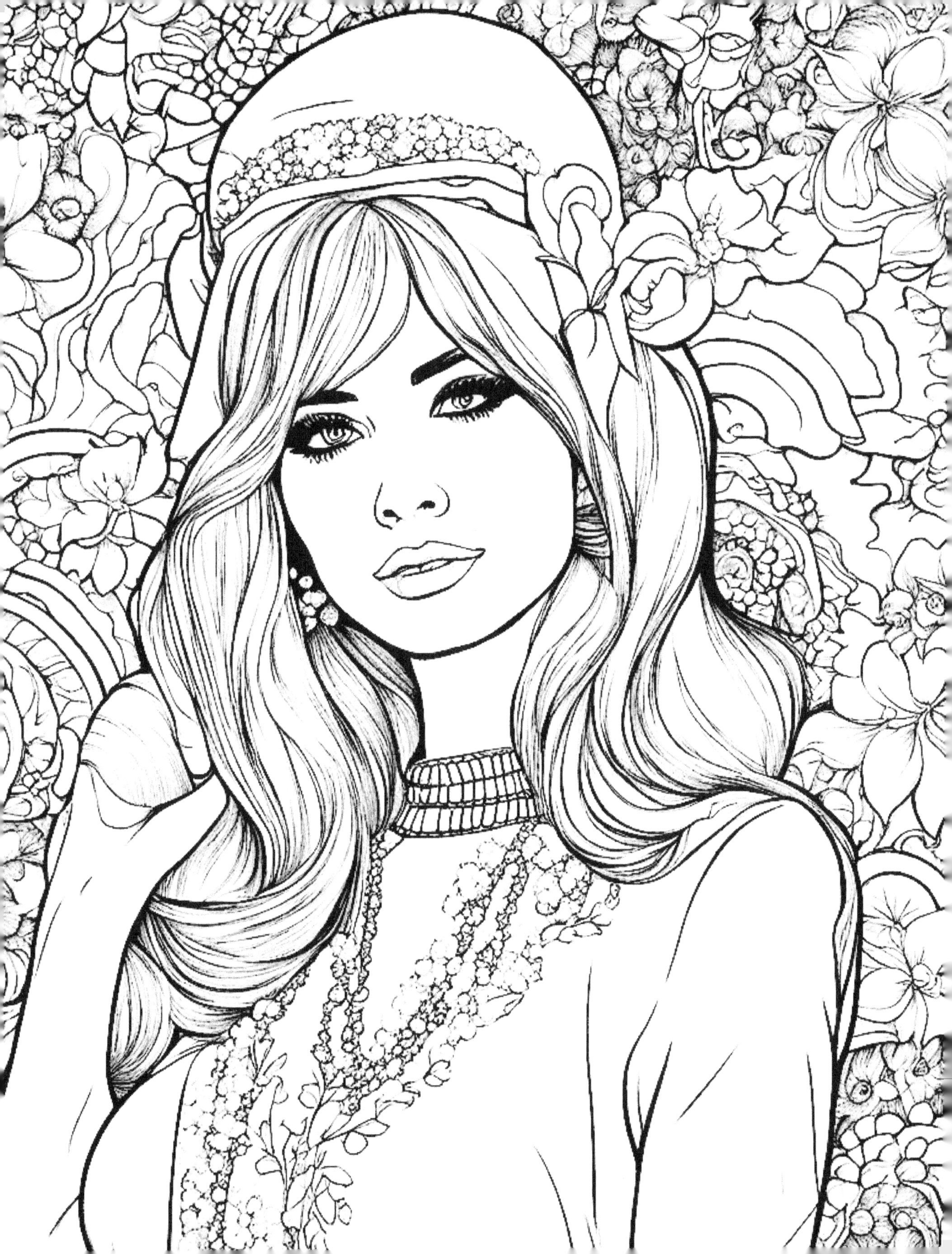

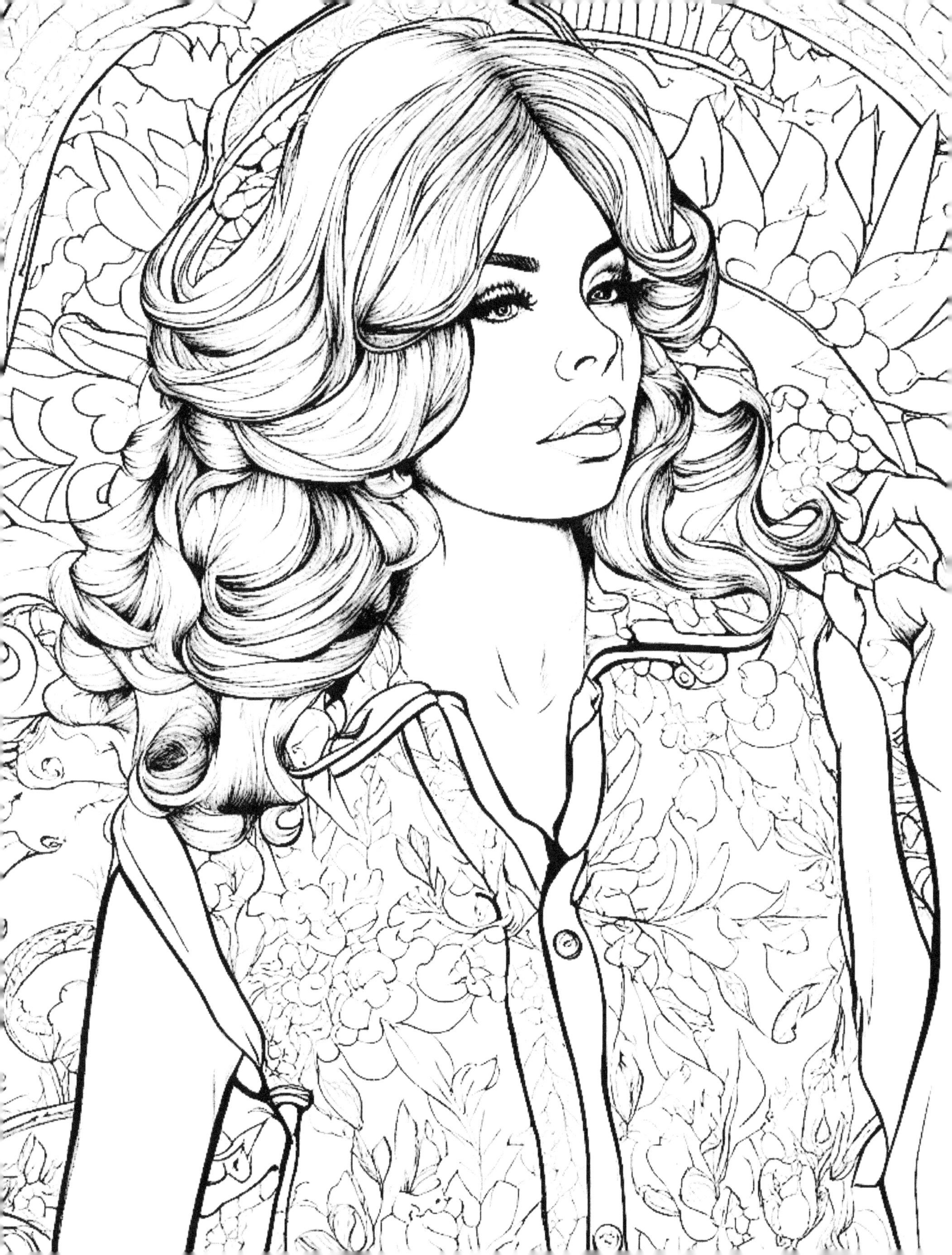

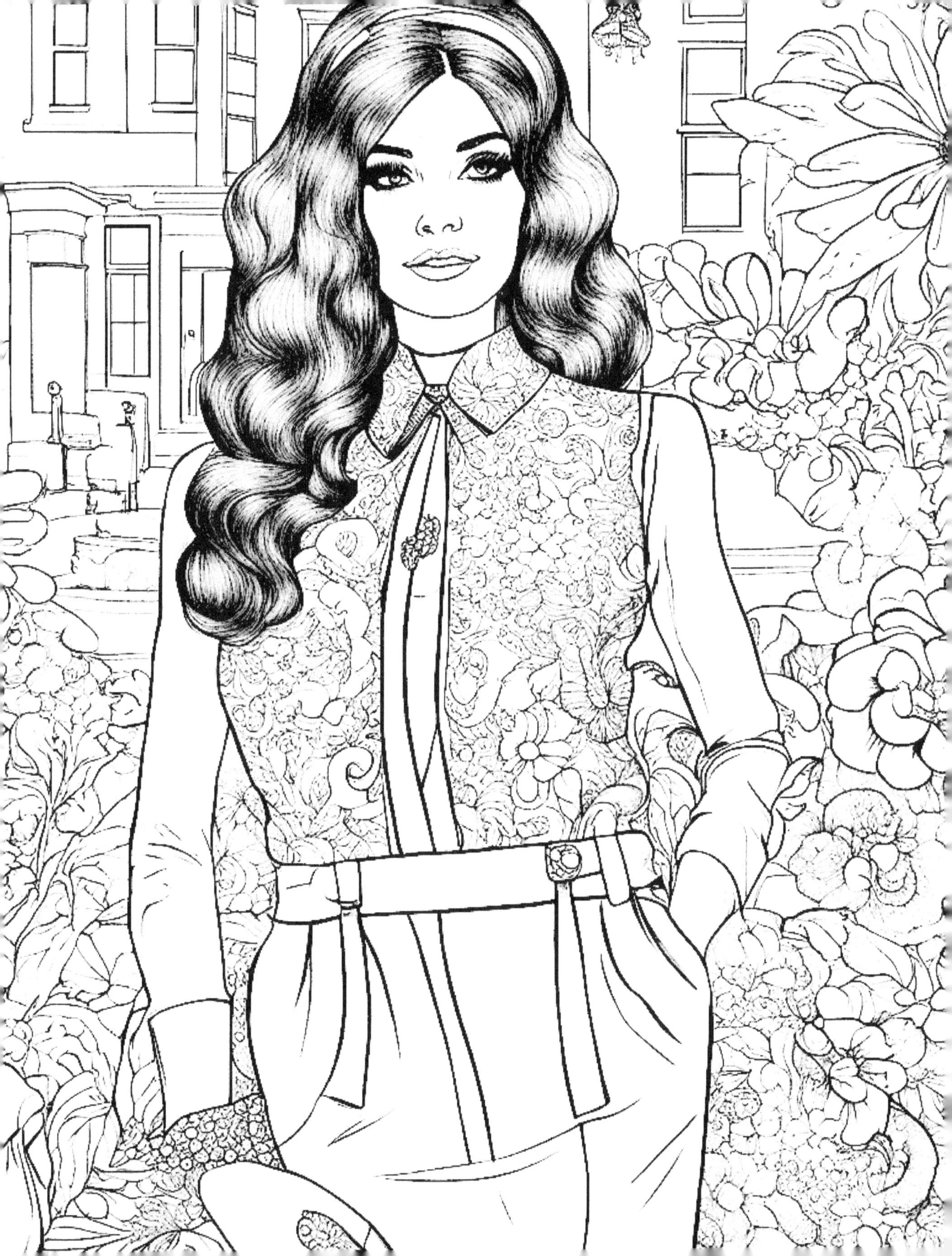

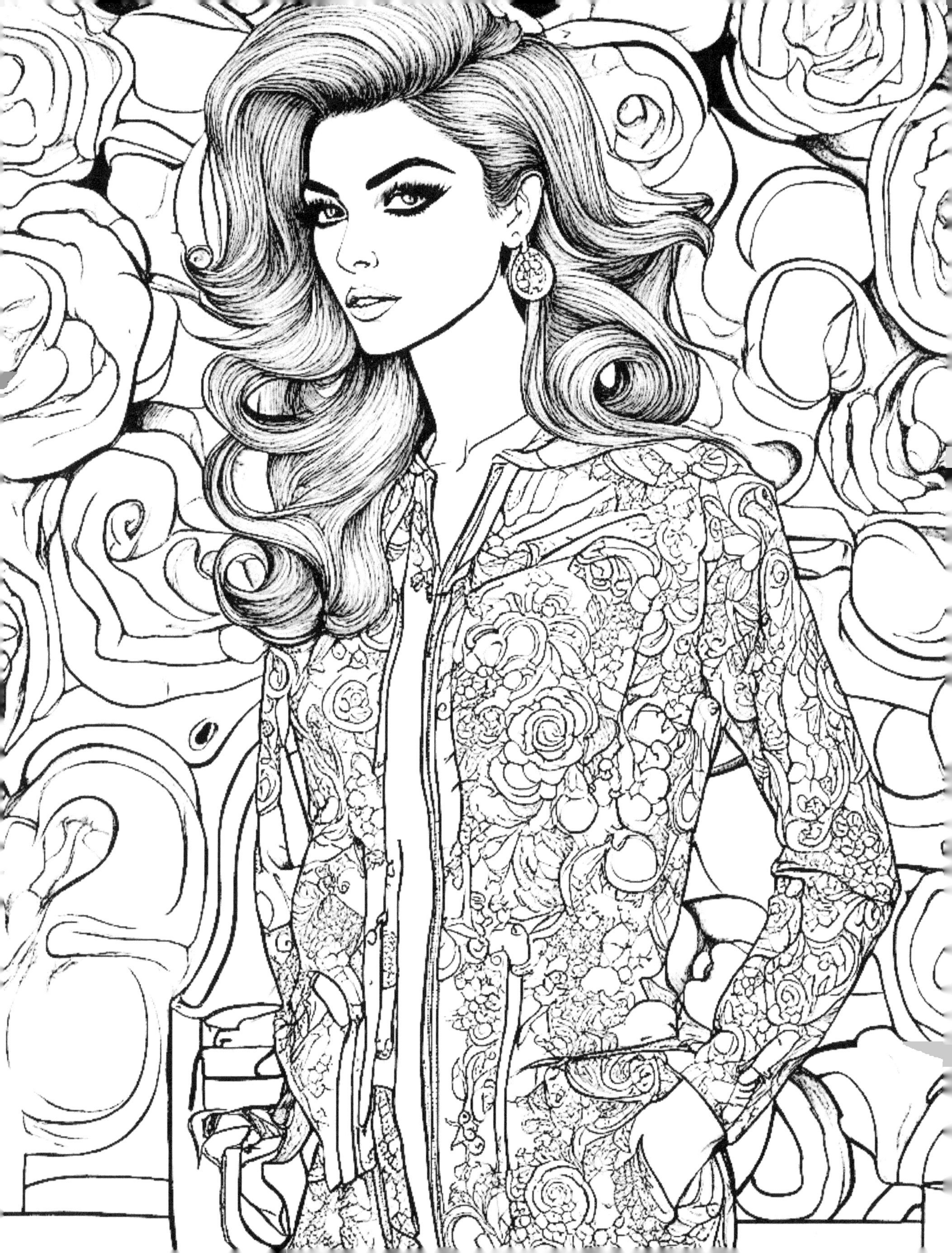

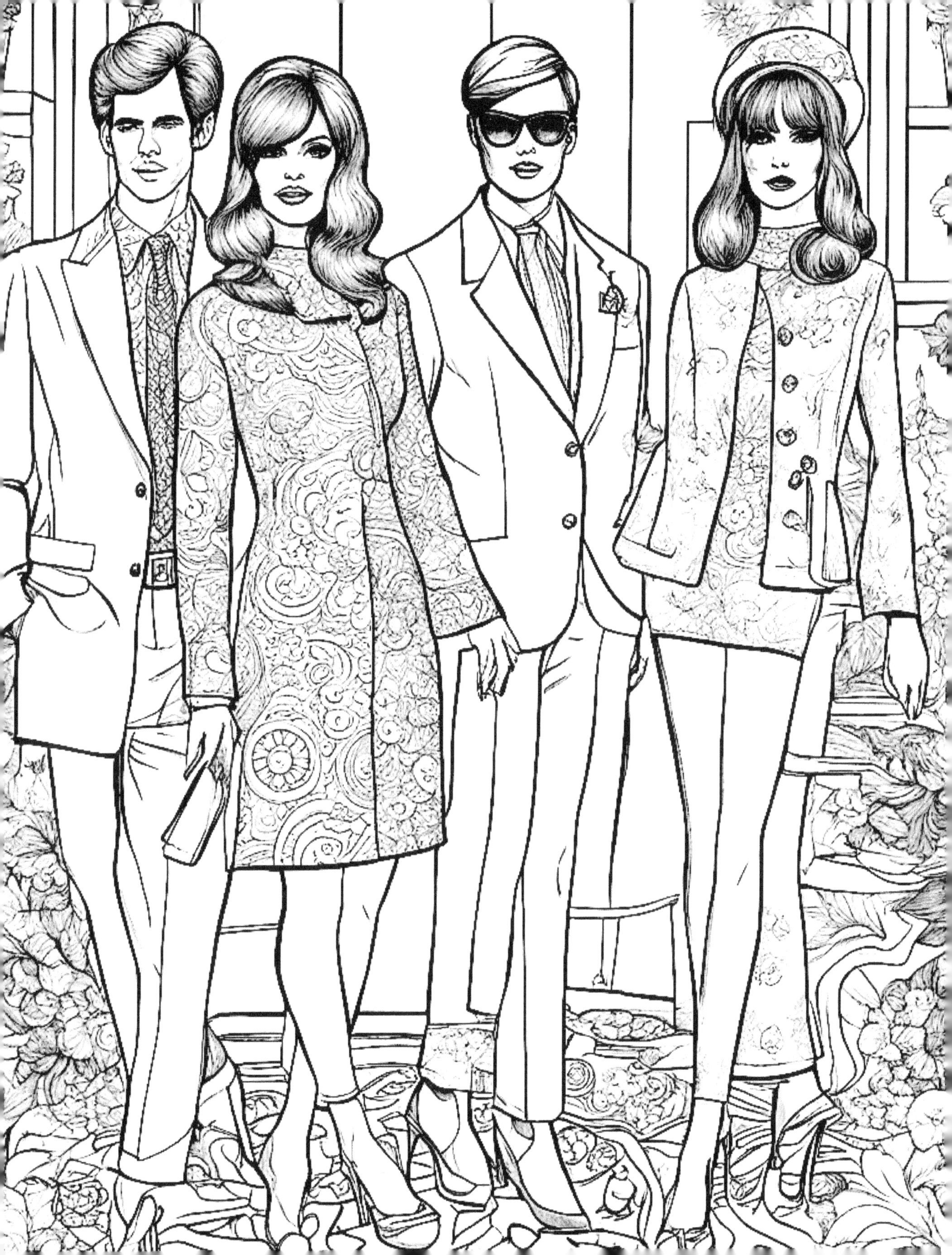

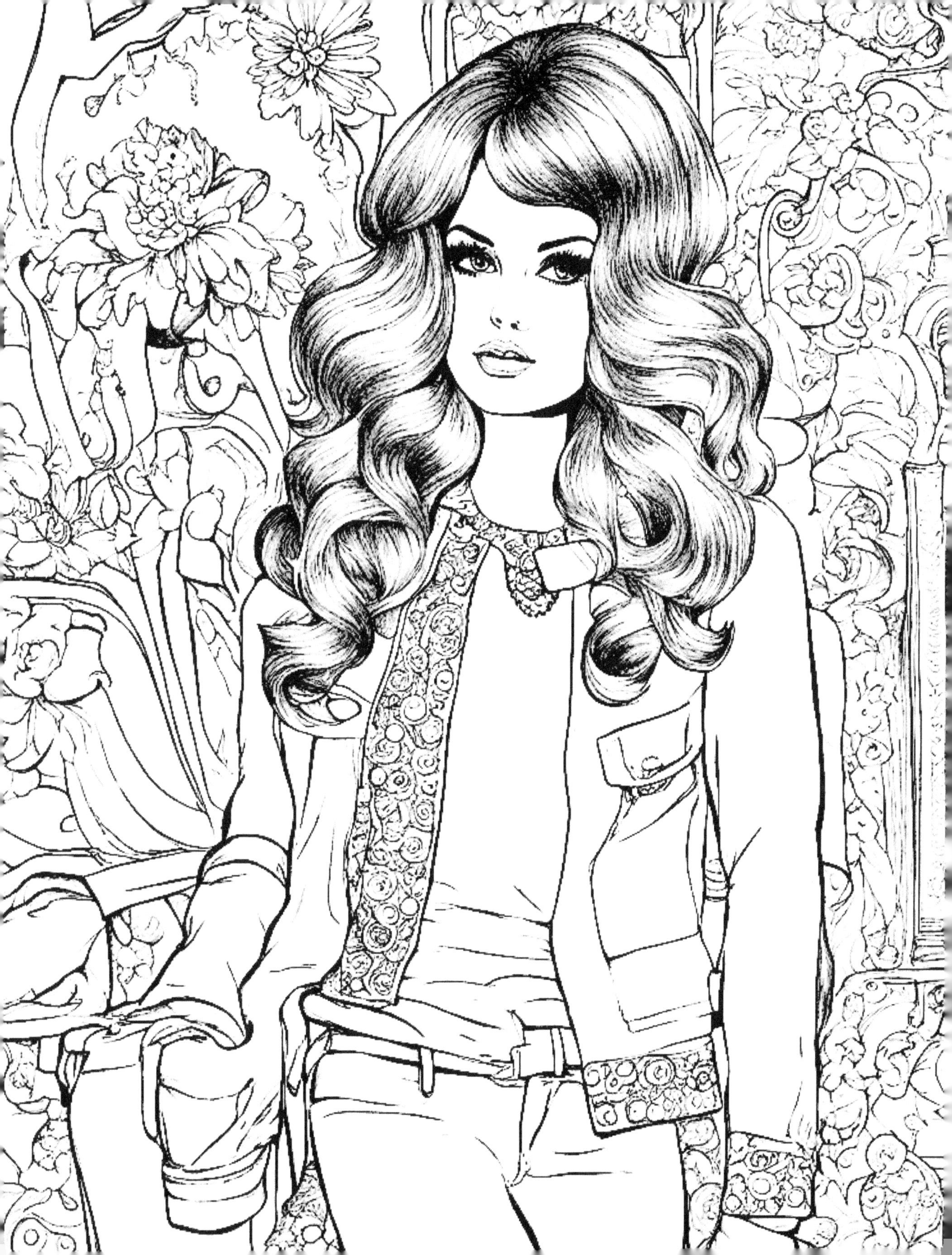

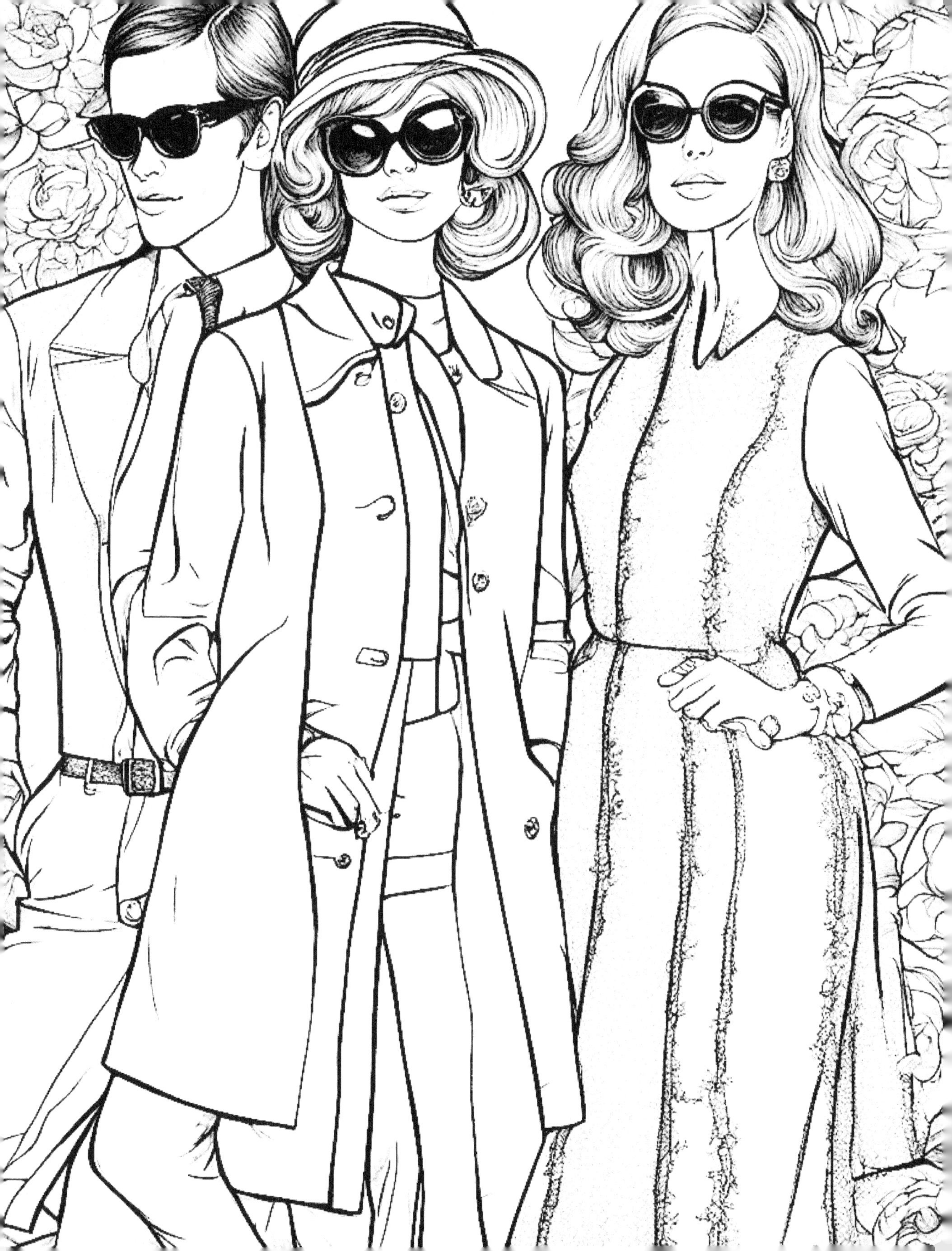

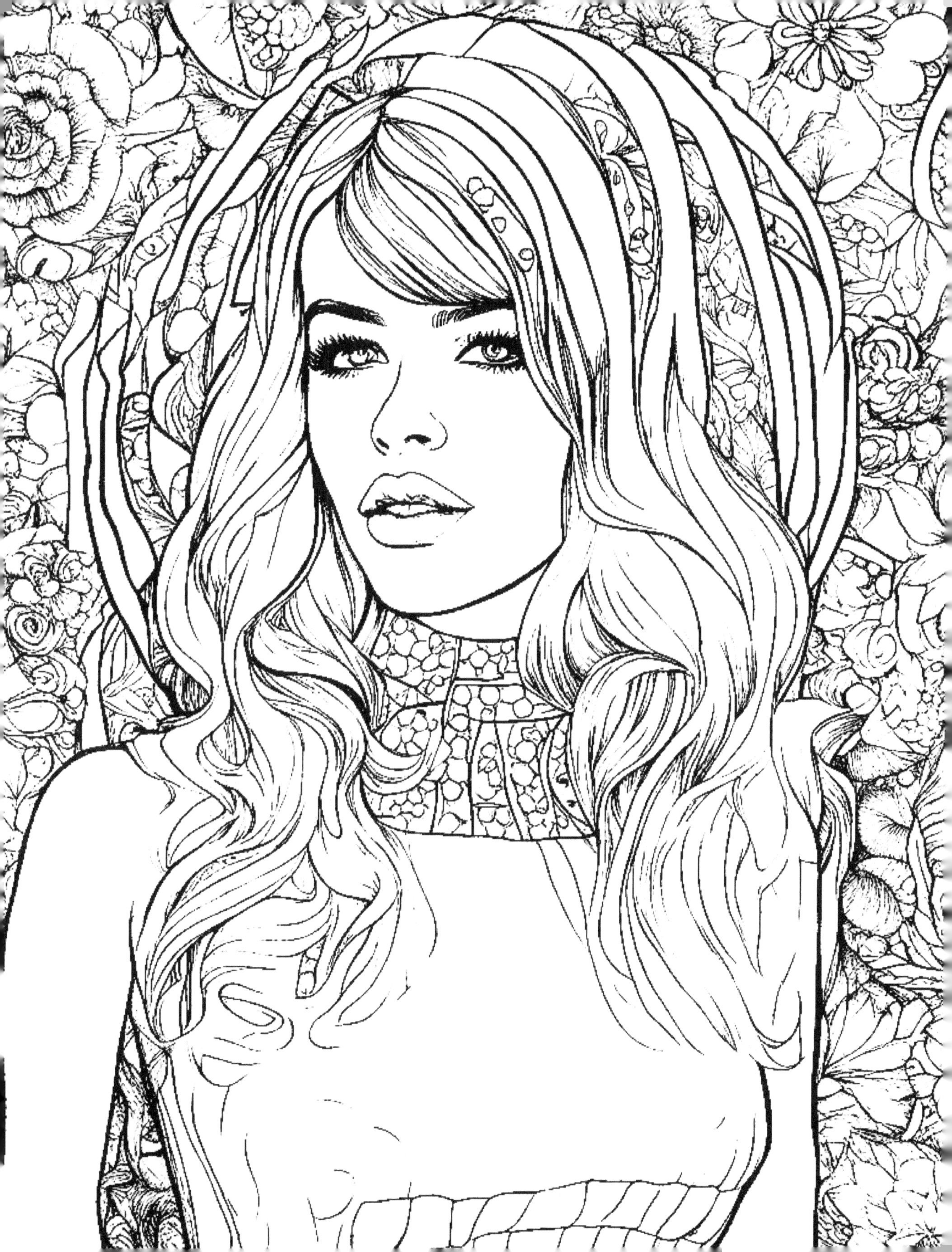

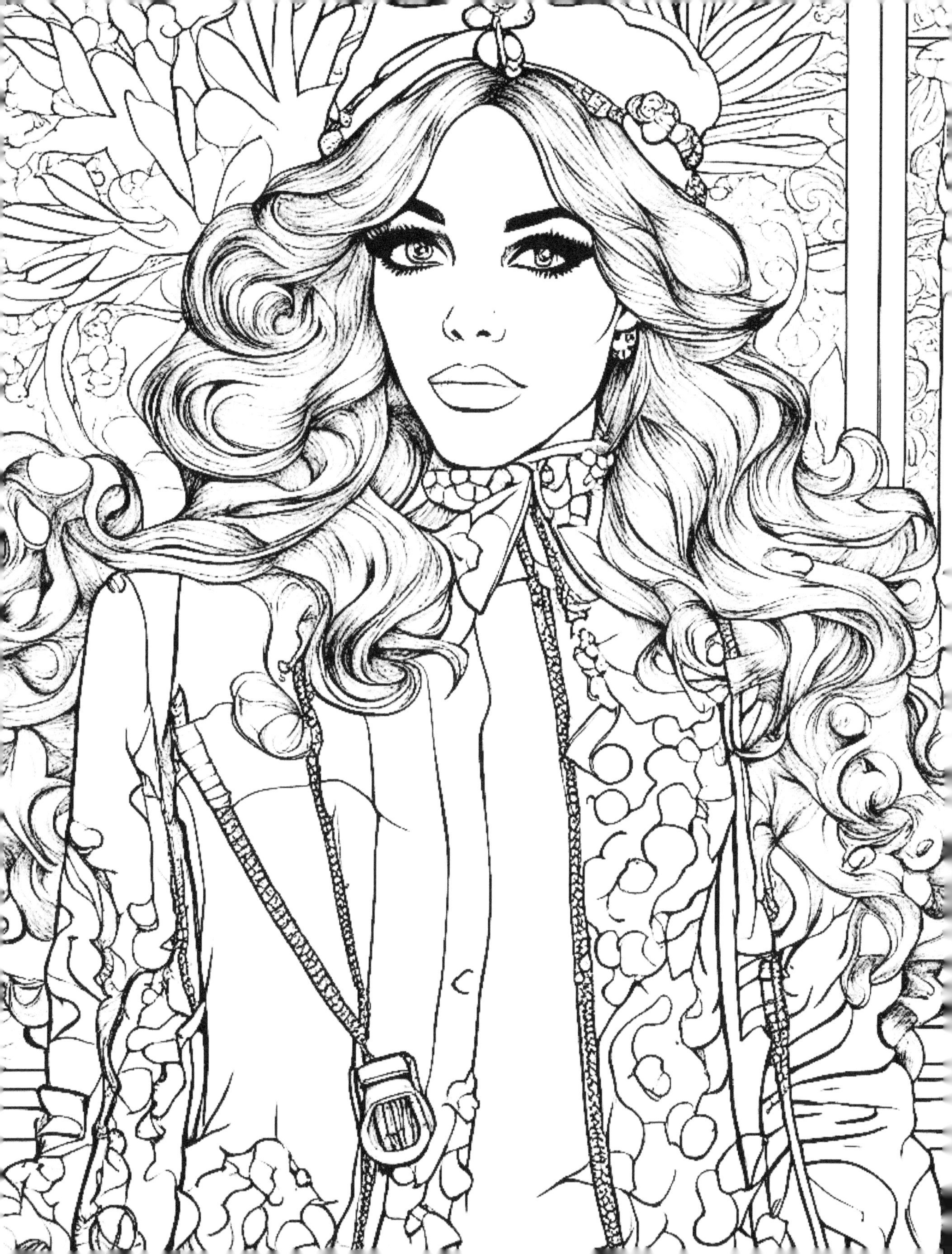

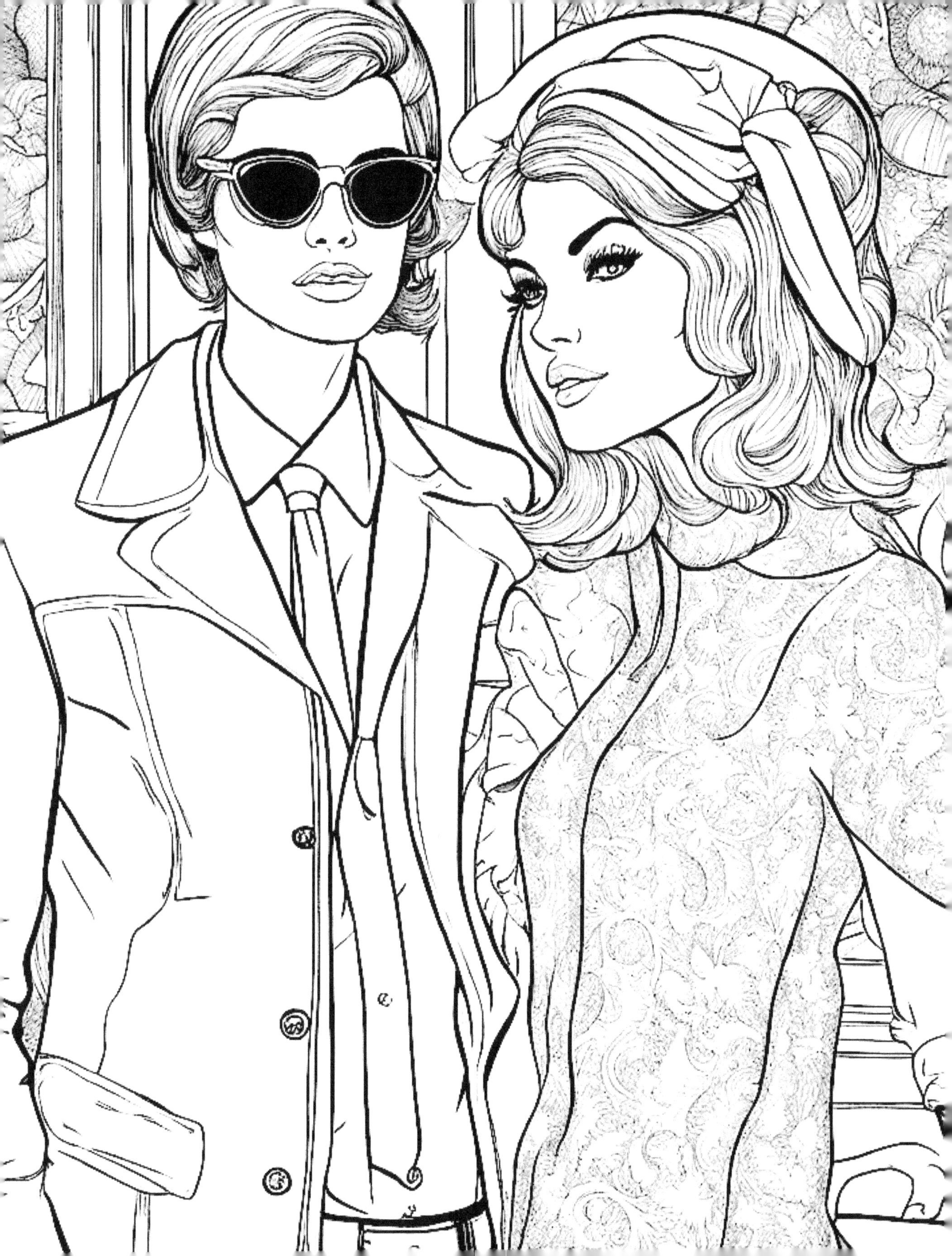

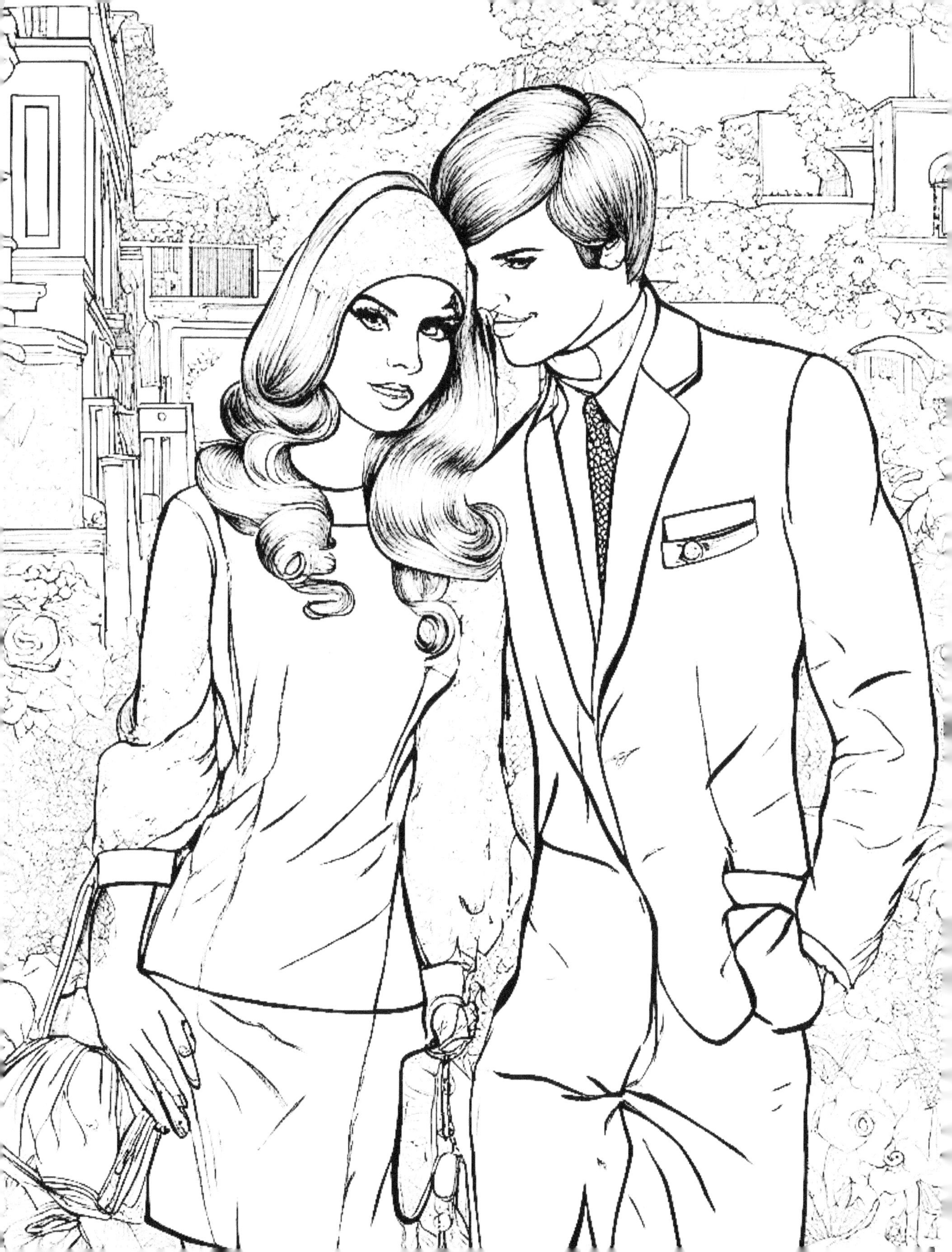

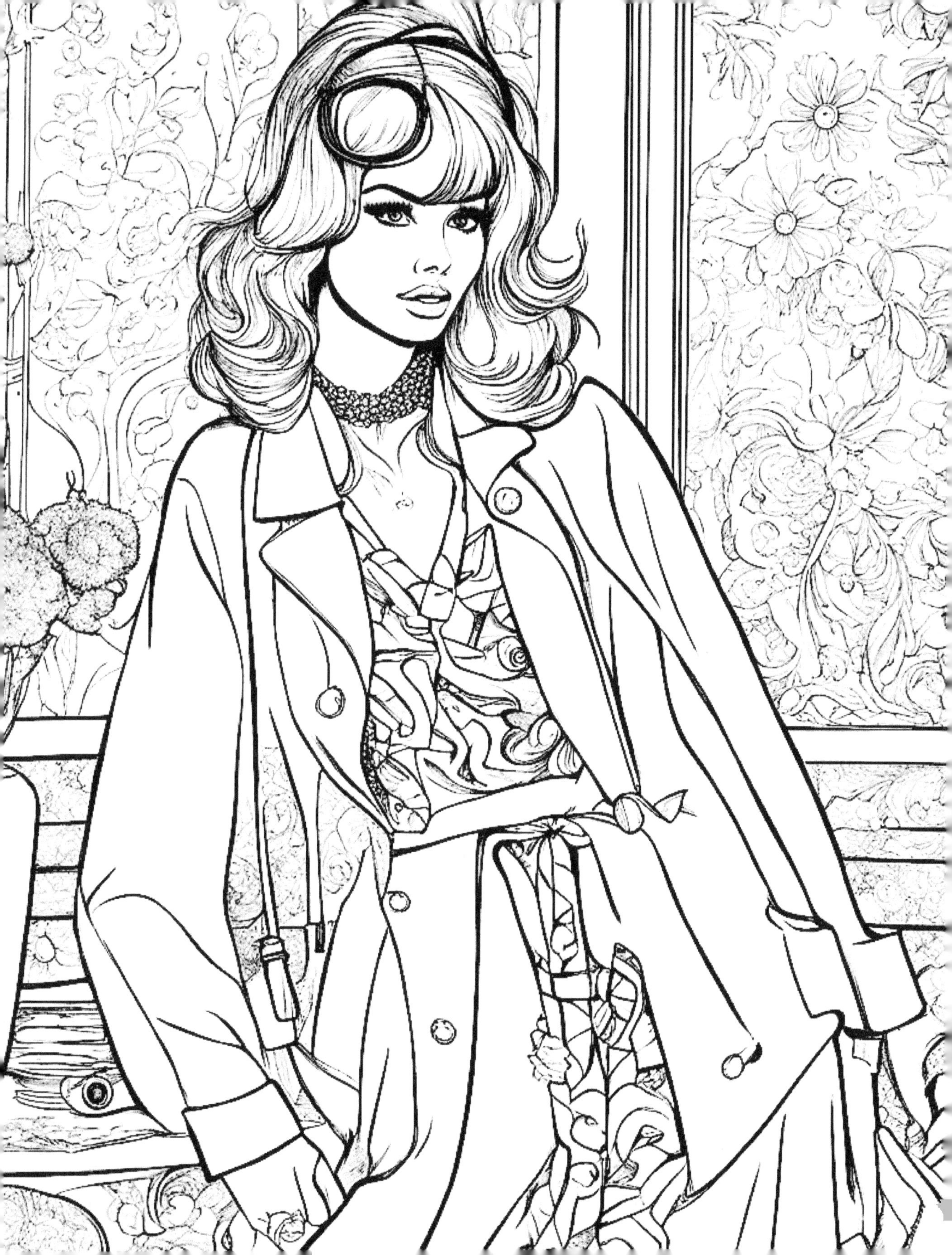

www.ingramcontent.com/pod-product-compliance
Lightning Source LLC
Chambersburg PA
CBHW081136290526
45795CB00006B/2257
9798883648976